THE PLAINT OF NULLITY AGAINST THE SENTENCE

THE CATHOLIC UNIVERSITY OF AMERICA
CANON LAW STUDIES
No. 360

THE PLAINT OF NULLITY AGAINST THE SENTENCE

A HISTORICAL SYNOPSIS AND A COMMENTARY

A DISSERTATION

Submitted to the Faculty of the School of Canon Law of the Catholic University of America in Partial Fulfillment of the Requirements for the Degree of Doctor of Canon Law

BY
REV. WILLIAM THOMAS CURTIN, A.B., J.C.L.
Priest of the Archdiocese of Kansas City in Kansas

THE CATHOLIC UNIVERSITY OF AMERICA
WASHINGTON, D.C.
1956

NIHIL OBSTAT:

Joannes Rogg Schmidt, J.C.D.
Censor Deputatus

Washingtonii, D.C. die 31 martii 1955

IMPRIMATUR:

✠Eduardus J. Hunkeler, D.D., LL.D.
Archiepiscopus Kansanopolitanus in Kansas

Kansasanopoli, die 11 aprilis 1955

Printed by
The Abbey Student Press, Atchison, Kansas

Respectfully Dedicated

with

Reverence and Gratitude

to

His Excellency

The Most Rev. Edward J. Hunkeler, D.D., LL.D.

Archbishop of Kansas city

in Kansas

TABLE OF CONTENTS

FOREWORD

The plaint of nullity stands in law as a remedy against the judicial sentence by which it is contended that the sentence is null for the reason that it labors under some substantial defect. It is the purpose of this dissertation to investigate the canonical institute known as the "*Querela Nullitatis contra Sententiam.*"

The plaint of nullity did not evolve in a simple way. The reasons for this fact seem to be either an internal conflict between the plaint of nullity and the sources of Roman Law, or the discrepancy between the Canon Law and the Civil Law. As a consequence, the plaint of nullity was not established as the proper and specific remedy against a sentence vitiated with nullity until the promulgation of the Code of Canon Law in 1918.

The present treatise is divided into two parts: the first will seek to furnish a synopsis of the historical development of the causes of nullity as attaching to the judicial sentence and as giving rise to a specific judicial remedy known as the *querela nullitatis*, and the second proposes to present a canonical commentary on the plaint of nullity in the measure that it can serve as a remedy against null judicial sentences.

The writer wishes to express his sincere gratitude to His Excellency, the Most Reverend Edward J. Hunkeler, D.D., LL.D., Archbishop of Kansas City in Kansas, for the opportunity of graduate study in Canon Law, and to the members of the Faculty of the School of Canon Law of the Catholic University of America for their kind assistance in the preparation of this work.

PART I

HISTORICAL SYNOPSIS

CHAPTER I

LEGISLATION PRIOR TO THE COUNCIL OF TRENT

Article I. Summary of Early Legislation

The plaint of nullity did not exist in Roman Law. If the sentence was null, it could be attacked by means of a declaration of nullity,[1] or by means of the exception of nullity.[2] Nullity in judicial processes was due to many causes in Roman Law. It could arise on the part of an incompetent judge, or on the part of disqualified parties, or also because of the deficient manner in which the trial was conducted, or finally, by reason of some infringing factor in the sentence itself.[3] Absolutely necessary were the citation, the joining of issue, the presence of the parties, except in a case of contumacy, a written sentence, and the presence of the parties at the pronouncement of the sentence.

In the early Church the remedy used against the nullity of a sentence was the appeal.[4] The plaint of nullity did not exist as an ordinary means of attacking a sentence vitiated with nullity. St. Gregory the Great (590-604) in an epistle to John, Bishop of Justiniana Prima,[5] declared that John's sentence against Bishop

[1] D (49.1) 19; C (1.14) 15. This process developed during the Formulary Period of Roman procedure.

[2] D (49.8)1; C (7.64) 1.

[3] C (50.1); C (64.1); Wenger, *Institutes of the Roman Law of Civil Procedure* (rev. ed., translated by Fisk, New York: Veritas Press, 1940), p. 309.

[4] Cf. c. 1, X, *de sententia et re iudicata*, II, 27.

[5] St. Gregorius Magnus, *Registrum Epistularum, Lib. III. ep.* 6 — *Monumenta Germaniae Historica, Gregorii I Papae Registrum Epistolarum*, Tomus I, pars I (ed. L. Hartmann, Berolini, 1891), pp. 163-165 (hereafter referred to as *MGH*); Jaffe, *Regesta Pontificum Romanorum ab condita Ecclesia ad annum post Christum natum* 1198 (2. ed., correctam et auctam auspiciis G. Wattenbach, curaverunt F. Kaltenbrunner, P. Ewald, S. Loewenfeld, 2 vols., Lipsiae, 1885-1888), n. 1210 (hereafter cited as JK, JE and JL).

Adrian of Thebes was absolutely invalid *ipso iure*. The case of Adrian came to John, Bishop of Justiniana Prima, on appeal from the court of John, Bishop of Larissa. The Bishop of Larissa[6] had condemned Adrian in regard to certain monetary causes, although Adrian was not within the jurisdiction of the Bishop of Larissa. John of Justiniana Prima confirmed the first sentence, and Adrian was deprived of his see. Against these two sentences, Adrian appealed to Pope Gregory. The Pope ordered Adrian's restoration to his see, and condemned the sentences of the Bishops of Larissa and of Justiniana Prima. Gregory in his epistle to John of Justiniana Prima made it clear that John's sentence, which was contrary to the laws and canons, could not have any existence in law, even if it had not already been suspended by an appeal. St. Gregory declared in his epistle that an unjust sentence was null and void *ipso iure*. The remedy used by Adrian was the appeal, which in this case was to be understood in a wide, untechnical sense.

After having treated of the time for and the renewal of appeals, Gratian (c. 1140) in his *Decretum* simply listed the causes of nullity of the sentence as found in Roman law. In these cases Gratian maintained that no appeal was necessary.[7]

Rufinus (+c.1190) declared that this was not true in regard to the courts of the Church, since the appeal was the remedy against a sentence which was null.[8] Stephen of Tournay (1128-1203), however, maintained that an appeal was necessary when the sentence was issued *contra ius litigatoris* (procedural law). If the sentence was given *contra ius constitutionis* (substantive law), the sentence was null and it was not necessary to appeal.[9]

Article 2. Nullity of the Sentence

There was no explicit mention of the *querela nullitatis* as such in the law of the Decretals (1234), nor was the *querela nullitatis*

[6] *Op. cit.* Lib. III, ep. 7, pp. 165-168; *JE*, n. 1211.

[7] *Dictum Gratiani*, post C. 41, C. II, q. 6.

[8] Rufinus, on c. 41, C. II, q. 6 — *Die Summa Decretorum des Magister Rufinus* (ed. H. Singer, Paderborn, 1902).

[9] Stephen of Tournay, on c.41, C. II, q. 6 — *Die Summa des Stephanus Tornacensis über das Decretum Gratiani* (ed. J. F. Schulte, Giessen, 1891).

considered at that time as the proper remedy against a sentence vitiated with nullity. In the writings of Durandus (+1296) and Bartolus (+1359), Pope Innocent III (1198-1216) was considered the author of this remedy — a remedy which was based on the application of definite principles of law.

The nullity of the sentence was more in evidence in Decretal law than in Roman Law. Decretal Law gave rise to more causes of nullity because of the distinction between the solemnities and the form on the one hand, and the judicial process itself on the other.[10]

Durandus recounted a long list of the various nullities as found enacted in the law of the Decretals.[11] He taught that a sentence was null: (1) on the part of the judge, if he was excommunicated,[12] or if he had incurred infamy,[13] or if a layman acted as a judge in things spiritual;[14] (2) from the jurisdictional approach, if the judge lacked jurisdiction over a case, e.g., if, when delegated for one thing he pronounces sentence concerning something else;[15] (3) on the side of the parties themselves, if the plaintiff (*actor*) was excommunicated,[16] or if a fictitious procurator acted for another in a case;[17] (4) in consideration of the place, if the judge issued a sentence outside his own territory[18] or if a civil judge issued a sentence in a church;[19] (5) in view of the element of time, if the sentence was issued at night, or after vespers, or on a festive day;[20] (6) in the light of the litigated cause, if the sentence did

[10] Wernz, *Ius Decretalium* (6 vols. in 10, Romae et Prati, 1898-1914), V. nn. 4-5; Roberti, *De Processibus* (2 vols. Romae: Apus Aedes Facultatis Iuridicae ad S. Apollinaris, 1926) I, n. 31.

[11] *Speculum Iuris* (Venetiis, apud Iuntas, 1577), lib. II, partic. III, *de sententia et re iudicata*, § 8.

[12] C. 24, X, *de sententia et re iudicata*, II, 27.

[13] C. 13, X, *de rescriptis*, I, 3.

[14] C. 3, X, *de iudiciis*, II, 1.

[15] C. 4, X, *de iudiciis*, II, 1; c. 3, X, *de consuetudine*, I, 4.

[16] C. 2, X, *de exceptionibus*, II, 25.

[17] Cc. 3, 4, X, *de procuratoribus*, I, 38.

[18] C. 1, *de foro competenti*, II, 2, in VI°.

[19] C. 2, *de immunitate, ecclesiarum, coemeteriorum et aliorum locorum religiosorum*, III, 23, in VI°.

[20] C. 5, X, *de feriis*, II, 9.

not absolve or condemn the party one way or the other;[21] (7) with reference to some qualitative factor, if the judge condemned the party but failed to specify the definite amount of payment due;[22] (8) in relation to the method or the manner, if the sentence was not drawn up in writing;[23] (9) by reason of manifest iniquity, if the sentence contained an express error,[24] or if it contravened the *ius scriptum*,[25] or if it demanded something impossible,[26] or if it was obtained through deceit,[27] and finally (10) from the procedural angle itself, if the sentence was issued without the joinder of issue[28] or if any procedural solemnity required by the law was omitted.

Moreover, Durandus declared that the serving of the citation, the introduction of the bill of complaint (*libellus*), the joinder of issue, taking of the called for oaths, and the pronouncement of sentence itself were absolutely necessary for a valid process.[29]

Article 3. Remedies in Law against the Nullity of the Sentence

1. Action and Exception of Nullity. In the law of the Decretals any sentence vitiated with nullity was invalid *ipso iure* and it had no force, even though it was not suspended by an appeal.[30]

The Decretal Law provided also for the exception of nullity against the sentence. Innocent III in 1207 declared that a trial was null and void since the mandate of the procurator had been

[21] C. 41, C. II, q. 6.

[22] C. 41, C. II, q. 6.

[23] C. 1, *de sententia, excommunicationis, suspensionis et interdicti*, V. 11, in VI°.

[24] Cc. 8, 9, X, *de sententia et re iudicata*, II, 27.

[25] C. 1, X, *de sententia et re iudicata*, II, 27.

[26] C. 7, X, *de conditionibus appositis in desponsatione vel in aliis contractibus*, IV, 5.

[27] C. 12, X, *de sententia et re iudicata*, II, 27.

[28] C. 1, X, *de litis contestatione*, II, 5.

[29] *Speculum Iuris*, lib. II in Summario ad partic. 1, nn. 1-2.

[30] C. 1, X, *de sententia et re iudicata*, II, 27. This was general law in the Decretals; the epistle of St. Gregory from which this was taken is discussed in Article 1 of this Chapter.

recalled, and though he had received notice of this revocation he nevertheless proceeded in the case. Innocent stated that the *exceptio falsi procuratoris* could be lodged not only before but also after the sentence, and if this exception was upheld then the judgment was null and void.[31] A sentence, however, that was invalid because of the presence in court of an unauthorized procurator could be ratified by the principal party through the giving of his consent to the sentence, provided that the sentence was void only because of this lack of consent.[32]

The law also recognized an action of nullity against a sentence vitiated with nullity. This action was introduced in the thirteenth century at the time of Innocent III according to the writings of both Durandus and Bartolus.

Moreover Durandus maintained concerning these points that a party could oppose the nullity of the sentence not only by way of a perpetual exception but also by way of an action of nullity which could be proposed within thirty or forty years unless some other provision obtained.[33]

The judicial action for the declaration of nullity was entered before the same judge who had issued the sentence.[34]

Durandus declared that, if the sentence was null, it was necessary that a new process be instituted for the judicial attack of the nullity. That meant a new bill of complaint, a new joinder of issue, and a repetition also of all the other acts.[35] Bartolus did not agree entirely with Durandus on this question. In answering the question whether the judge could pronounce on the nullity from the same record, Bartolus contended that if the defect which

[31] C. 4, X, *de procuratoribus*, I, 38; A. Potthast, *Regesta Pontificum Romanorum inde ab anno post Christum natum* 1198 *ad annum* 1304, (2 vols., Berolini, 1874-1875), n. 2995.

[32] Abbas Panormitanus (Nicholaus de Tudeschis, 1386-1453), *Commentaria in Quinque Libros Decretalium* (5 vols. in 7, Venetiis, 1588), lib. II, tit. 27, *de sententia et re iudicata*, c. 1, n. 22 (hereafter cited as *Commentaria*).

[33] *Speculum Iuris*, lib. II, partic. III, *de sententia et re iudicata*, §8, nn. 27 and 30.

[34] Cf. *Glossa*, ad c. 1, *de sententia et re iudicata*, II, 11, in Clem., s.v. *agendum de nullitate*; Durandus, *Speculum Iuris*, lib. II, partic. III, *de sententia et re iudicata*, §8, n. 27.

[35] *Speculum Iuris*, lib. II, partic. III, *de sententia et re iudicata* §8, n. 26.

caused the nullity of the sentence concerned equally the acts as well as the sentence, then all the acts had to be repeated in the trial. The example he gave was that of a trial in which a minor did not have a guardian. If the cause of nullity was concerned only with the sentence, e.g., the sentence was pronounced on a festive day, then the cause could be adjudged from the same record.[36]

In the practice of the Papal Curia, however, it was necessary to enter a new process or suit in pleading nullity against the sentence.[37]

2. Simple Petition. A remedy which was very commonly adverted to in the Decretals was the presenting of a simple petition to the judge who had issued the sentence that was vitiated with nullity. He could issue another sentence if he then saw that the first sentence was invalid.

Durandus declared that it was the practice of the Curia that a judge who had ordinary power should commence from the beginning and amend his sentence. He could then issue a second sentence if he knew that the first sentence was wrong. Moreover, Durandus stated that the ordinary judge, once he noted that he had issued a null sentence, could issue another sentence without a new bill of complaint or without any other retraction.[38]

Hostiensis (+1271) maintained that if the ordinary judge issued a sentence which was null *ipso iure*, he himself could revoke it and issue another sentence; if he was a delegated judge, he could not change it, inasmuch as his office ceased with the issuing of the sentence.[39]

Baldus (+1400) declared that not only the ordinary judge, but

[36] Bartolus a Saxoferrato (+1359), *Commentaria*, Tomus VIII, *In Secundum atque Tertiam Codicis Partem*, (Venetiis, 1590), ad septimum librum Codicis, tit., *de sententia, et interlocutionibus omnium iudicum*, lex 4, n. 5 [or C (7.43) 4].

[37] Durandus, *Speculum Iuris*, lib. II, partic. III, *de sententia et re iudicata*, § 8, n. 26.

[38] *Speculum Iuris*, lib. II, partic. III, *de sententia et re iudicata*, §5, n. 10, and §8, n. 27.

[39] Hostiensis (Henricus de Segusio), *In Quinque Libros Decretalium Commentaria* (5 vols., Venetiis, 1581), Lib. II, *de sententia et re iudicata*, c. 1, n. 4.

likewise the delegated judge could issue a new sentence if the first sentence was null. Baldus maintained, however, that in accordance with the current laws the delegated judge had to enjoy a general delegation, and not simply a delegation *ad causam*.[40]

On this same subject, Panormitanus asked the question whether or not a judge could pronounce a sentence a second time when the first sentence was null. He answered that an ordinary judge could issue another sentence, but not the delegated judge, unless there was question of a probable error.[41]

In his *Summa*, Hostiensis also declared that upon petition the judge could retract or amend the sentence. Among the various possibilities discussed, Hostiensis considered the contingency of a sentence which was grammatically false. In this event the judge could amend his sentence. In another instance, a party who had been absent was condemned; accordingly, when this absent party proved that his absence was legitimate, the sentence had to be retracted. Also discussed by Hostiensis was a contingency in which an ecclesiastical benefice had been obtained through deceit or acquired illicitly. There, too, the judge could retract his sentence. In matrimonial causes, if the sentence was null *ipso iure* or deserved to be annulled because of an error of fact, the sentence could be retracted by the ordinary judge, or also by the delegated judge when he had the necessary authority.[42]

3. The Appeal. Moreover, a sentence vitiated with nullity could be remedied by means of an appeal according to law.[43] The Decretals of Gregory IX repeated the laws of Justinian on the question of appeals. The twenty-eighth title of the second book of the Decretals corresponds to that of the forty-ninth book of the Digest.

All could appeal who reasonably considered themselves injured by a sentence. They were not to be excluded from using such a

[40] Baldus, *Additio* to the *Speculum Iuris* of Durandus, lib. II, partic. III, *de sententia et re iudicata*, p. 809.

[41] *Commentaria*, II, *de sententia et re iudicata*, c. 1 n. 25.

[42] *Summa Aurea* (Venetiis, 1570), tit., *De sententia et re iudicata*, parag. *Quot sint*, s.v. *Diffinitiva*.

[43] C. 15, X, *de appellationibus, recusationibus, et relationibus*, II, 28.

remedy.[44] No appeal was allowed a party if the object in litigation had become a matter adjudged (*res iudicata*), or if the right to appeal had been renounced.

The right to appeal was denied if a cause had been committed to a judge with the words *appellatione remota* attached.[45] If, however, the Pope delegated the judge to try a cause *appellatione remota*, then there were precluded only those appeals which were not expressly permitted by law.[46] It was likewise not possible for a person who had lost a judicial suit in consequence of his contumacy to make an appeal.[47] He had a remedy, however, in his plea for reinstatement in prior status, the *restitutio in integrum*.

Decretal Law was explicit in stating that the appeal had to be filled within a space of ten days after the sentence was pronounced. This was based on the *Decretum Gratiani*.[48]

The appeal, however, could be made *viva voce* immediately after the sentence was issued, or it could be made in writing within the period of ten days.[49] Moreover, it was necessary that the party who was to appeal have knowledge of the sentence before the ten-day period could begin. This period was not to be shortened or lengthened by the judge.[50]

The number of appeals in the hearing of a judicial cause was limited to two. This number was always allowed even if the appellate judge was delegated by the Pope himself.[51]

In discussing this question of appeals, Bartolus declared that the appeal could be used against the nullity of a sentence. He maintained that this appeal could be effective, if the nullity was considered as distinct from the injustice of the sentence. Because of the injustice of a sentence, the judge could change or rectify

[44] Cc. 7, 10, 72, X, *de appellationibus, recusationibus, et relationibus*, II, 28.

[45] C. 41, X, *de appellationibus, recusationibus, et relationibus*, II, 28.

[46] C. 47, X, *de appellationibus, recusationibus, et relationibus*, II, 28.

[47] C. 8, X, *de officio iudicis ordinarii*, I, 31.

[48] C. 15, X, *de sententia et re iudicata*, II, 27; C. 28, C, II, q 6.

[49] C. 34, X, *de appellationibus, recusationibus et relationibus*, II, 28; c. 15, X, *de sententia et re iudicata*, II, 27.

[50] C. 15, X, *de sententia et re iudicata*, II, 27; Durandus, *Speculum Iuris*, lib. II, partic. III, *de appellationibus*, parag. 5, nn. 1-2.

[51] C. 65, X, *de appellationibus, recusationibus, et relationibus*, II, 28.

the sentence provided he did not admit the nullity. If, however, he did admit the nullity, he had to state this and then allow the appeal to drop, or at most he was to say that the appeal did not hold.[52]

4. *Restitutio in Integrum.* In addition to the plaint of nullity and the appeal, another remedy used against the nullity of a sentence was the *restitutio in integrum.* The reason for admitting this remedy was that the Decretalists themselves could not agree on all the causes of nullity. Even those stated by Durandus caused a certain amount of injustice. This injustice in sentences that were vitiated with nullity was also the reason, no doubt, that the use of appeal against the nullity of sentences was granted.

Durandus likewise maintained that just as one could propose an appeal against the nullity of the sentence, so one could oppose the sentence by way of the *restitutio in integrum.*[53] Bartolus agreed to this. He declared that this was actually the practice of the Curia, since in the seeking of the *restitutio in integrum,* there was a certain hope of defense, and custom approved that practice.[54]

Restitutio in integrum, as a remedy of law, was first established by the Roman praetors. They used it in such causes which involved persons still in their minority, or absent parties, or when the element of force and fear, or a factor such as error, attended the suit.[55]

The *restitutio in integrum,* as a judicial remedy against the sentence or a transaction, was definitely established in ecclesiastical procedure by Alexander III (1159-1181).[56] It was considered as an extraordinary remedy that was used only when no ordinary remedy proved permissible and available. It was best defined in the *Glossa* of the Decretals as "a restoration to previous status or right." Ordinarily this remedy was not employed against invalid acts; but, as was explained above, the nullity of the sentence

[52] Bartolus, *Commentaria,* in: C. (7.64) 1, n. 8, VIII, 86; D (49.1) 19, n. 4, VI, 200.

[53] *Speculum Iuris,* lib. II, partic. III, *de sententia et re iudicata,* §8, n. 28.

[54] *Commentaria,* in: D (49.1) 19 — n. 9, VI, 200.

[55] D (4.4) 17; D (4.4) (1.1); D (4.1) 8; D (4.2) 1; D (4.1) 2.

[56] C. 1, X, *de in integrum restitutione,* I, 41.

could easily be doubtful, and hence this remedy was *de facto* used.

This remedy was granted to minors in the courts of the Church;[57] and because a church as a juridic entity and personality had the same rights in this regard, the *restitutio in integrum* was also available to a church.[58] Other parties could use this extraordinary remedy only if all other remedies were lacking and a just reason existed for its use, such as a procurator's neglect in a case.[59]

The great advantage of the *restitutio in integrum* was evident in those cases in which no appeal had been made within the ten-day period and the sentence had become a matter adjudged (*res iudicata*), or also when a person had lost the right to appeal because of contumacy.[60]

For minors the period within which this remedy could be used was four years after the completion of the twenty-fifth year of age; for churches the period was the same space of four years, but counted from the time the sentence had been issued or the transaction was completed.[61] This remedy had to be initiated for its use before a judge who had the proper authority. He had to be competent.

Concerning the effects of the *restitutio in integrum*, the sentence was to be relinquished as if not pronounced and the transaction was to be disregarded as if never reached. The parties involved were restored to their previous status or rights.[62]

5. Cumulative Petition. In the attacking of a sentence vitiated with nullity, a cumulative petition was also permitted. The use of it evolved in consequence of the numerous sources of nullity, their subtleness, and the lack of agreement among the Decretalists themselves on the causes of such nullities. In such contingencies the petition would seek all the remedies — plaint of nullity, appeal, and *restitutio in integrum*. The use of these

[57] C. 8, X, *de in integrum restitutione*, I, 41.

[58] Cc. 1, 3, X, *de in integrum restitutione*, I, 41.

[59] Panormitanus, *Commentaria*, II, *de sententia et re iudicata*, c. 7, n. 12; c. 1, X, *de in integrum restitutione*, I, 41.

[60] C. 8, X, *de officio iudicis ordinarii*, I, 31.

[61] C. 1, *de restitutione in integrum*, I, 21, in VI°; Hostiensis, *Summa Aurea*; *De in integrum restitutione*, n. 4.

[62] C. 4, X, *de in integrum restitutione*, I, 41.

cumulative petitions is exemplified in the Decretals themselves.[63]

Durandus declared that such cumulative petitions were admitted by the Curia, and that Pope Clement VI (1265-1268) had even commissioned him to receive these petitions and to exercise his judgment and decision regarding them.[64]

6. *Supplicatio.* There was another extraordinary remedy allowed in Decretal Law. This was the *supplicatio*, which could not be employed as long as there were other remedies available. This remedy allowed the petitioner to approach the Pope with the request that he permit the case to be tried again. This remedy, if granted, always demanded a new process.

Panormitanus maintained that the granted use of *supplicatio* evinced an act of kindness on the part of the superior, by means of which the superior retracted all those things which he believed to be evil.[65]

If anyone doubted whether or not he could appeal in a given contingency, he could *ad cautelam* seek both remedies—the appeal and the *supplicatio*. The *supplicatio*, however, differed from the appeal. The *supplicatio* was an extraordinary remedy, whereas the appeal was an ordinary remedy. As a result, the *supplicatio* could never be employed whenever an appeal could still be made.

Panormitanus stated that if the right to appeal had been lost to a party, nevertheless that party could still use the *supplicatio* against the sentence. He declared further that these were two separate processes, one an ordinary remedy and the other an extraordinary remedy. He concluded that the loss of one did not mean the loss of the other.[66]

The appeal had to be made within the ten-day period; the *supplicatio*, if made to the *princeps*, could be proposed within the space of two years. Nothing could be changed in a cause during the time that the appeal was pending. The opposite was true in the event that a *supplicatio* had been interposed.[67] According to

[63] C. 8, X, *de in integrum restitutione*, I, 41; c. 14, X, *de privilegiis*, V, 33.

[64] *Speculum Iuris*, lib. II, partic. III, *de sententia et re iudicata*, §8, n. 27.

[65] *Commentaria*, I, *de restitutione in integrum*, c. 4, n. 6.

[66] *Commentaria*, I, *de restitutione in integrum*, c. 4, nn. 3, 9.

[67] Panormitanus, *Commentaria*, I, *de restitutione in integrum*, c. 4, n. 12. cf. *Glossa*, ad c. 4, X, *de in integrum restitutione*, I, 41, s.v. *supplicavit*.

Durandus, the *supplicatio* could be made but once, whereas the appeal could be made twice in the seeking of redress.[68]

7. *Querela.* In the Decretals, *Querela* was still another remedy available for use against a sentence. It seems that during its period of development the *querela* was used in the rehearing of cases which were concerned with the status of persons — causes dealing with the factor of excommunication and relating to the bond of marriage.

The *querela* was always directed to the judge who had issued the sentence, and not to the Pope. The *Glossa* declared that the *querela* was to be lodged before the same judge who had issued the sentence, and if the sentence was not yet irrevocably adjudicated, the judge could retract the sentence.[69]

This same *Glossa* stated that, if the party had not used his right to appeal within the ten-day period, then this right was lost. Moreover, he could not implement the *querela* through the appeal; but the party still could lodge a simple *querela* by itself in order to place a complaint against the sentence even after the ten-day period.

Panormitanus maintained that after the time for an appeal had expired, a redress could still be sought by way of a *querela* if the object in controversy had not been irrevocably adjudicated. This remedy was addressed to the same judge who had issued the sentence. If, however, the party had used his right to appeal within the ten-day period, then the hearing of the cause had to be carried to the appellate court, and the *querela* could not be lodged.[70]

Hostiensis declared that a simple *querela* was to be directed, not to the appellate court, but always to the judge who had issued the sentence.[71]

If the *querela* was lodged against a sentence vitiated with nullity, the judge was not unconditionally to admit the use of this

[68] *Speculum Iuris*, lib. 11, partic. III, *de supplicationibus*, parag. 3, n. 3.

[69] Cf. *Glossa*, ad c. 8, X, *de officio iudicis ordinarii*, I, 31, s.v. *suspendatur*.

[70] *Commentaria*, I, *de officio iudicis ordinarii*, c. 8, n. 6 and n. 12.

[71] *Commentaria*, I, *de officio iudicis ordinarii*, c. 8, n. 5.

remedy, but he was first to examine the cause in at least a summary manner.[72]

In conclusion, the law of the Decretals declared: (1) that the nullity of a sentence could be countered with the perpetual exception of nullity; (2) that the nullity of a sentence could be countered with a nullity suit which could be entered within thirty or forty years unless some other proviso was made; (3) that the entry of a judicial suit as also the raising of an exception of nullity took place before the same judge who had issued the sentence. In the proposing of the plaint of nullity, however, the practice of the Roman Curia demanded a new process; (4) that another commonly available remedy was the simple petition presented to the judge who had issued the null sentence, that he recall or retract that sentence, and (5) that a sentence vitiated with nullity could be variously remedied by way of an appeal, a *restitutio in integrum*, also a cumulative petition, a *supplicatio*, and, finally a simple *querela*.

The plaint of nullity did not exist as the exclusive remedy against a sentence vitiated with nullity. This remedy did exist, however, in the law of the Decretals. If a sentence was null, it was left to the party to decide which of the remedies he wanted to use in the circumstances surrounding the litigated cause.

[72] Panormitanus, *Commentaria*, II, *de sententia et re iudicata*, c. 10, n. 6 and c. 11, n. 9.

CHAPTER II

HISTORICAL DEVELOPMENT FROM THE SIXTEENTH CENTURY

ARTICLE 1. NULLITY OF THE SENTENCE

When Pope Pius IV (1559-1565) reformed the tribunal of the Sacred Roman Rota in 1561, he declared that thenceforth but three classes of nullities were to be admitted: nullity arising from a defect in jurisdiction, or from the omission of the proper citation, or from the lack of a sufficient mandate by a procurator.[1] The following year this same legislation was extended by Pius IV to include the Signatura and the other tribunals of Rome.[2] This legislation was confirmed again in 1612 by Paul V when he reformed the Roman tribunals.[3]

Scaccia (in 1604) when speaking of the restrictions to be placed on nullities, declared that notorious nullities which can be proved immediately from the acts were not to be rejected or eliminated. His reason for this statement was that the restrictions were concerned only with the nullities *per modum excipiendi* or *per modum agendi* and not with manifest nullities that vitiated the sentence.[4]

De Luca (1614-1683) praised the Apostolic Constitutions for restricting the causes of nullity in judicial acts inasmuch as these Constitutions excluded the nullities that arose from a too rigorous insistence on the formalities of procedure. De Luca also explained that, for the nullity to emerge it was not postulated that the defect in jurisdiction, in the citation, or in the mandate of the procurator be directly evident; rather the particular circumstances in

[1] Const. *In Throno Iustitiae*, 1561, §13 — *Bullarum Diplomatum et Privilegiorum Sanctorum Romanorum Pontificum Taurinensis Editio* (24 vols., et Appendix, Augustae Taurinorum, 1857-1872), VII, 155 (hereafter cited as *Bull. Rom.*).

[2] Const. *Cum ab Ipso*, 1562 — *Bull. Rom.*, VII, 214.

[3] Const. *Universi Agri*, 1612, 5, n. 19 — *Bull. Rom.* XII, 68.

[4] *Tractatus de Appellationibus* (3 ed., Coloniae, 1717), Quaestio XIX, Rem. I, Concl. IV, nn. 44-45.

each case were to be taken into account and subjected to a due appraisal.[5]

Outside the Papal States, the restrictions on procedural nullity did not hold for several centuries, but many other causes were considered sufficient grounds for nullity. As a result, the question regarding the factor of nullity became intensified in its import. One of the best sources evidencing this growth was the work by Maranta (c. 1530). He gave at least thirty cases in which a judicial process became *ipso iure* invalid.[6]

The tendency to multiply the causes of nullity was continued by Altimarus (1638?-1713). This author gave as general categories of nullity: defect of jurisdiction, ordinary or delegated; defect or disqualification in the parties themselves or in those who represented the parties; defect of citation; defect in the trial itself; defect or solemnity or form in the sentence; and nullity in respect to the execution of the sentence.[7]

Beginning with the classical commentators, however, one notes the trend to restrict the causes of nullity. Gonzalez-Tellez (fl. 1673) stated that these causes were various and that they were still numerous. He explained that these nullities could arise on the part of the judge, on the side of the parties, or through the manner in which the trial was conducted. Gonzalez-Tellez declared that a sentence was null by reason of manifest injustice when procedural law had been violated.[8]

Reiffenstuel (1642-1703) repeated the enumeration of the causes of nullity as found in Ioannes Andreae (1275?-1348). These causes, nine in number, derived from the following factors and elements: the person of the judge, the parties, the place, the

[5] *Theatrum Veritatis et Iustitiae* (16 vols., Coloniae Agrippinae, 1706) VII, disc. 38, n. 22, 177.

[6] *Speculum Aureum et Lumen Advocatorum Praxis Civilis* (Venetiis, 1590), pars. IV, dist. 16.

[7] *Tractatus de Nullitatibus in XIV Rubricas Divisus* (Neapoli, 1678), Rub. II, n. 1.

[8] *Commentaria Perpetua in singulos textus quinque librorum Decretalium Gregorii* IX (5 vols., Venetiis, 1756), lib. II, tit. 27, c. 9, n. 1 (hereafter cited *Commentaria*).

quantity, the time, the process, the manner, the manifest iniquity, and the attendant condition.[9]

Schmalzgrueber (1663-1735) listed three causes of nullity: (1) nullity caused through a defect of capacity (*capacitas*) or ccmpetence (*competentia*) in the judge — either the judge was not capable of jurisdiction, or, though he was capable, he did not possess jurisdiction, or its use was impeded; (2) nullity caused through a defect in the parties — either one of the parties did not have the right to appear in court, or the procurator did not have a valid mandate, or his mandate had been recalled or had expired, and (3) nullity caused through the failure to observe the necessary order in the trial — the proper sequence was not observed.[10]

The commentators of this earlier period made a distinction between intrinsic and extrinsic validity of the sentence in its requisite solemnities.

For the intrinsic validity of the sentence the following things were required: (1) the judicial sentence had to conform to the law, both the substantive and the procedural law; (2) the sentence had to relate properly to the bill of complaint; (3) the sentence had to be definitely specific, containing either a condemnation or an absolution; (4) the sentence had to be absolute and independent of contingent conditions; (5) the sentence could not be based on false testimony either manifest or readily demonstrable as such.[11]

For the extrinsic validity of the sentence it was necessary: (1) that the parties be cited; (2) that the sentence be expressed in writing and read by the judge to the exclusion of others; (3) that the judge be seated in the place of the tribunal, not standing or walking about; (4) that the sentence be issued during the day time, and also on a day that was not a court holiday (*in die non feriato*).[12]

[9] *Ius Canonicum Universum* (5 vols. in 6, Romae, 1831-1834), lib. II, tit. 27, n. 72 (hereafter cited as Reiffenstuel).

[10] *Ius Ecclesiasticum Universum* (5 vols. in 12, Romae: 1843-1845), lib. II, tit. 1, n. 78 (hereafter cited as Schmalzgrueber).

[11] Reiffenstuel, lib. II, tit. 27, nn. 70-97; Schmalzgrueber, lib. II, tit. 27, nn. 37-40.

[12] Reiffenstuel, lib. II, tit. 27, nn. 58-64; Schmalzgrueber, lib. II, tit. 27, nn. 50-61.

These distinctions were very important in the development of restrictions on the causes of nullity.

The customs of the place and the established curial practice (*stylus curiae*) of the individual tribunals were to be considered in this matter, even through the common law predicated nullity for the sentence *ipso iure* if there were omitted the solemnities which responded to the requirements for extrinsic validity.[13]

In the Papal States, the restrictions on the nullities of the sentence as they were first determined by Pius IV and Paul V in regard to the Rota and the other tribunals were confirmed from time to time by other Pontiffs.[14]

During this same period of the eighteenth and nineteenth centuries, the Congregation of the Council added the weight of its authority in the continuing restriction of the causes of nullity. The Sacred Congregation of the Council declared the sentence of an appeal court invalid because the citation had been omitted and the acts of the process had not been sent to the court of second instance.[15]

Again, in 1746, this same Congregation set aside as invalid a sentence of excommunication inflicted in consequence of an alleged violation of the privilege of the canon. The reasons that were presented in the petition to this Congregation revealed that the judge lacked jurisdiction, that the citation had been completely omitted, and that the sentence was unjust because the privilege of the canon had not actually been violated.[16]

[13] Reiffenstuel, lib. II, tit. 27, n. 69.

[14] Clemens XII (1730-1740), Const., *In summi pontificatus specula*, 1734—*Bull. Rom.* XXIV, 11; Clemens XIII (1758-1769), const., *Ex parte*, 1759, § 10 — *Bullarii Romani Continuatio* (18 vols; Romae, 1835), I, 348; Benedictus XIV (1740-1758), const., *Iustitiae et pacis custodes*, 1746 — *Bullarii Romani Continuatio* (13 vols. Prati, 1846), II, 137; Pius VII (1800-1823), *Quando per ammirabile disposizione*, 1816, n. 47 — *Bullarii Romani Continuatio* (Prati), XII, 1274; Gregorius XVI (1831-1846), *Elevati appena per divino volero*, 1834, n. 780 — *Bullarii Romani Continuatio* (Romae), XIX, 467.

[15] S.C.C., *Lucana*, 2 et 16 dec. 1719 — *Codicis Iuris Canonici Fontes*, cura Emi Petri Card. Gasparri editi (9 vols., Romae: Typis Polyglottis Vaticanis, 1923-1939; vols. VII-IX, ed. cura et studio Emi Iustitiani Card. Serédi), n. 3196 (hereafter cited as *Fontes*).

[16] S.C.C., *Albintimilien*, 18 iun. 1746 — *Fontes*, n. 3586.

Wernz (1842-1914) declared that a sentence issued by a judge could be invalid either because of incompetence or because of some other disqualification of the judge or of the parties, or because there was not observed the essential form in the canonical procedure, e.g., the citation was omitted or, in matrimonial causes, the defender of the bond (*defensor vinculi*) was not summoned, or finally because the rendered decision was contrary to the clear and certain meaning of the law or the judicial acts.[17]

Lega (1860-1935) explained that an act was truly null by the natural law when some substantial element was lacking, e.g., if an error touched the very substance of the act. Likewise, an act was null by the positive law if it lacked the form which this law prescribed for the validity of the acts. These two principles held for all acts, judicial and extrajudicial. In regard to the validity of exclusively judicial acts, Lega maintained: (1) that an act which was valid by the natural law or labored under no substantial defect, though it was forbidden by the positive law, was to be considered equally valid according to the positive law, unless it was expressly forbidden under pain of nullity; (2) that in a doubt whether or not an act that was valid by the natural law was likewise valid by the positive law, the general principle, namely that in doubt an act is assumed as valid, was to be invoked; (3) that the canons which prescribed certain acts for validity had essentially to be observed, e.g., Benedict XIV in his Constitution *Dei miseratione*, in 1741, had under pain of nullity required the presence of the defender of the bond in all matrimonial causes; (4) that, even though the law did not explicitly demand a certain requisite act for the substance of the process, nevertheless the trial was null if the act was omitted, e.g., if the defendant was not given the right to defend himself, since this denial of right was contrary to the natural law; (5) that at times the omission or the imperfect performance of some act rendered the whole process null according to the inherent nature of the particular procedural act, and (6) that the nature of the process and the purpose of the judicial instance had to be investigated if one was to determine whether

[17] *Ius Decretalium* (6 vols. in 10, Romae et Prati, 1898-1914, V. lib. I, n. 709 (hereafter cited as Wernz).

or not some act had to be drawn up in a certain form for the validity of the process.[18]

When the Rota was reinstated in 1908, the rule was imposed on this tribunal that the sentence was "*sub poena nullitatis*" to be written in Latin and was to contain the reasons, both of fact and of law.[19]

In a later edition of the *Regulae servandae* of the Rota, this regulation was again confirmed; but its text omitted mention of the necessity of writing the sentence in Latin.[20]

Moreover, in the *Regulae servandae* of the Apostolic Signatura of 1912, the rules indicated what served as grounds for the plaint of nullity: (1) a lack of the citation by which the cause was introduced; (2) the absence of jurisdiction; (3) a lack of, or substantial error in, the procurator's mandate; (4) the failure, in the sentence, to taking cognizance of some law; (5) any manifest violation of law.[21]

Article 2. The Plaint of Nullity against the Sentence

In the development of the *querela nullitatis contra sententiam* prior to the Council of Trent, there was no universal law or regulation which established any specific remedy for the nullity of the sentence. The practice of the various tribunals allowed the nullity of the sentence to be attacked by means of the plaint of nullity, by way of a cumulative appeal, or through the plea for a *restitutio in integrum*. These were the principal remedies permitted.

Section 1. Early Practice of the Roman Curia

When Pope Pius IV reformed the Sacred Roman Rota in 1561, he listed the three classes of nullities that would vitiate a sentence. In his Constitution the Pope mentioned the appeal and the *resti-*

[18] Lega, *De Iudiciis Ecclesiasticis* (4 vols., Romae, 1896-1901), Vol. I, lib. 1, nn. 250-251.

[19] *Lex propria S. R. Rota et Signaturae Ap.*, 29 iun. 1908, can. 32, § 3—*Fontes*, n. 6459.

[20] *Regulae servandae in iudiciis apud S. R. Rota Tribunal*, 4 aug. 1910, § 182 — *Fontes*, n. 6461.

[21] *Regulae servandae in iudiciis apud Supremum Signaturae Ap. Tribunal*, 6 mart. 1912, art. 4 — *Fontes*, n. 6462.

tutio in integrum, but said nothing concerning the plaint of nullity against the sentence.[22] This same trend in regard to the plaint of nullity was found in succeeding papal constitutions.[23]

The Sacred Roman Rota employed the plea for a *restitutio in integrum* as the proper remedy against a sentence vitiated with nullity. This practice continued during the sixteenth and seventeenth centuries. The nullity or the injustice of the sentence was regarded as constituting the postulated detriment that sufficed for the use of this extraordinary remedy.[24] The result of this procedure in the Roman Curia was that the plaint of nullity was no longer employed.

DeLuca (1614–1683) in speaking of the Roman tribunals stated that the plaint of nullity had all but ceased to exist in the Roman Curia.[25] This jurisprudence of the Roman Curia and especially of the Rota was reflected in the writings of Gonzales-Tellez. This author included many examples of nullity vitiating the sentence in his commentary on the *restitutio in integrum*, and thus seemed to state that the *restitutio in integrum* was the proper remedy.[26] DeLuca maintained that the practice of the Rota looked to the *restitutio in integrum* as the proper remedy to be used in correction of a null sentence.[27]

Gonzales-Tellez, however, declared that an exception of nullity could be raised if the nullity resulted from the acts themselves; but in all such cases the exception of nullity could not be proposed

[22] Const., *In Throno Iustitiae*, 1561 — *Bull. Rom.*, VII, 155.

[23] Const., *Cum ab Ipso*, 1562 — *Bull. Rom.*, VII, 214; const., *Universi Agri*, 1612 — *Bull. Rom.*, XII, 68.

[24] *Decisiones Recentiores* (19 parts in 25 vols., Franco-furti-Aureliae-Romae, 1623-1703), I, dec. 492, n. 1 (1613); XVIII, tom. 2, dec. 740, n. 1 (1676).

[25] "In Tribunalibus Rotae . . . huius remedii exercitium principaliter ab aula recessisse videtur." — *Theatrum Veritatis et Iustitiae*, VII, disc. 38, n. 5.

[26] Gonzales-Tellez, *Commentaria*, lib. I, tit. 49, c. 6.

[27] ". . . adeo ut saepissime, peneque millies in Rota disputaverim super consueto dubio, an constet de re iudicata, vel potius de causis restitutionis in integrum, nunquam vero disputaverim, neque disputatum viderim principaliter super hoc dubio, an constet de nullitatibus." — *Theatrum Veritatis et Iustitiae*, VII, disc. 38, n. 5.

against a matter already adjudged (*res iudicata*).[28] On this same point DeLuca held that an exception of nullity could be lodged against a null sentence before that sentence was executed, the proper remedy was *manutensio*, which was but a form of the plea for a *restitutio in integrum*.[29]

The procedure of the Rota and of the other Roman tribunals in not employing the plaint of nullity was due most likely to the restrictions imposed on the causes of nullity affecting the sentence. This practice, however, of not using the plaint of nullity was not observed in tribunals outside the Papal States. DeLuca seemed to intimate as much when he wrote concerning the disputes over nullities that took place in other tribunals.[30]

Section 2. The Classical Commentators

The plaint of nullity was employed when a party impugned the sentence of nullity because of some substantial defect. The plaint of nullity could be proposed either by way of a suit in court or by way of an exception in the suit.[31]

Reiffenstuel defined the plaint of nullity in these words: *Oppositio nullitatis sententiae, est legitima ostensio sententiam a iudice latam esse ipso iure nullam.* This opposing plea of nullity was usually made in the manner of a complaint (*per viam querelae*).[32]

Reiffenstuel in explaining a simple plaint (*querela*) declared that the plaint was employed in causes that had not become irrevocably adjudicated. After the lapse of ten days, a sentence of this kind could be revoked or recalled, not by way of an appeal, but only by way of a plaint. The plaint was proposed to the same judge who issued the sentence, not to the judge of appeal. In all causes of nullity, however, the plaint could likewise be proposed to the appellate judge if the party preferred to approach him.

[28] *Commentaria*, lib. II, tit. 27, c. 9.

[29] *Theatrum Veritatis et Iustitiae*, VII, disc. 38, nn. 5-6.

[30] DeLuca, *ibid.*, n. 6.

[31] Pichler (1670-1736), *Ius Canonicum* (Ravennae, 1741), lib. II, tit. 28, n. 5 (hereafter cited as Pichler): Schmier (+1728), *Ius Canonicum Universum* (Venetiis, 1754), lib. II, tract 3, c. 13, nn. 192-193 (hereafter cited as Schmier).

[32] Reiffenstuel, lib. II, tit. 28, n. 23.

Before accepting the plaint in court, the judge before whom the sentence had been rendered was to make a preliminary investigation concerning the justice of the plaint and the injustice of the sentence; and then, having recognized the truth, the judge was to retract the sentence.[33]

In all causes that never became irrevocably adjudged, Reiffenstuel declared that, if the defect could be validated by the party, the plaint was to be proposed within ten days, for otherwise it was presumed that the defect had been validated.[34]

It was clear and certain that the plaint of nullity could be invoked in either of two ways, namely as an independent issue (*principaliter*), or as an incidental one (*incidenter*). The plaint of nullity could be invoked *principaliter* either cumulatively with an appeal (*dico sententiam nullam, et si quae est appello*), or separately and by itself.

The plaint of nullity could be invoked *incidenter* either by way of an appeal, inasmuch as this remedy tacitly implied the cause of nullity in itself, or also by way of a judicial exception. Furthermore, it could be utilized for the purpose of having the judge pronounce a new sentence in order to rule out the earlier null sentence, and finally when the nullity was manifest or notorious.[35]

Schmier (+1728) maintained that the plaint of nullity against the sentence could be invoked principally either with an appeal, upon a charge that the sentence was null or at least unjust; or separately and by itself, in which case it was invoked before the judge who pronounced the sentence. This same author stated that as a plea invoked incidentally by way of appeal, no express mention of the nullity being made, the nullity of the sentence had to be investigated *ex officio* by the judge, if the nullity was evident from the judicial acts.[36]

[33] Reiffenstuel, lib. II, tit. 27, nn. 135-138; cf. *supra*, chapter I, n. 7, p.

[34] Reiffenstuel, lib. II, tit. 27, nn. 120-125.

[35] Pellegrini (+1678), *Praxis Vicariorum* (Venetiis, 1706), pars III, sect. 1, n. 64 (hereafter cited as Pellegrini); Pichler, lib. II, tit. 28, n. 5; Engel, *Collegium Universi Iuris Canonici* (9. ed., Beneventi, 1760), lib. II, tit. 28, n. 5 (hereafter cited as Engel).

[36] Schmier, lib. II, tract 3, c. 13, nn. 193-194; cf. Pellegrini, pars III, sect. 1, n. 65.

Of what interest however, was it whether the plaint of nullity was invoked principally or only incidentally before the appellate judge? If the plaint of nullity was invoked principally, and the plaintiff failed in his proof, he could not invoke again the remedy of appeal, but was condemned to pay the expenses, and the sentence was sent back for execution to the judge who rendered it.

If the plaint of nullity was invoked only incidentally as included in an appeal, then even though the appeal failed, the plaintiff could still maintain that the sentence was null, and the appellate judge was accordingly obliged to take cognizance of the nullity.[37]

The plaint of nullity could be proposed either before the same judge who had issued the sentence, provided he was a judge with ordinary power, or the plaint of nullity could be proposed before the appellate judge, if it was introduced as a new and independent suit.[38]

In explaining the differences between an ordinary judge and a delegated judge before whom a sentence vitiated with nullity could be opposed, Reiffenstuel maintained that an ordinary judge could *de iure* reform his sentence which was null and could issue another sentence. The plaint of nullity could be invoked separately and by itself, as when there was a plea that the sentence be pronounced null and then reformed, also incidentally, as when one of the litigants sought the pronouncement of a sentence again in a cause and thus introduced the plaint of nullity as an intermediate issue. Moreover, Reiffenstuel cautioned that if the plaint of nullity was invoked only incidentally, then the appellate judge could not be approached, since the plaint was not lodged by way of an appeal nor by way of an independent suit or primary issue.

The practice quite definitely pointed to the superior judge as the one who was approached. The plaint of nullity was of course being invoked as a separate primary suit, especially if the nullity had arisen through the malice or turpitude of the judge of original jurisdiction, and not through an error.[39]

[37] Engel, lib. II, tit. 28, n. 5; Pichler, lib. II, tit. 28, §1, n. 7 and § 3, n. 16.

[38] Reiffenstuel, lib. II, tit. 27, n. 138; lib. II, tit. 28, n. 28; Pellegrini, pars II, sect. 3, subsect. 1, n. 90; pars III, sect. 1, n. 64; Engel, lib. II, tit, 28, n. 3.

[39] Reiffenstuel, lib. II, tit. 27, n. 138; lib. II, tit. 28, nn. 29, 31.

Engel (+1674) set forth the same opinion when he declared that the plaint of nullity could be invoked either before the judge who issued the sentence or before the appellate judge, and that the latter should be approached when the nullity arose not through the element of error, but in consequence of the malice of the judge of the lower court. The reason was that the judge of the lower court could not readily be expected to acknowledge his malice.[40]

Schmalzgrueber (+1735) did not mention the malice of the judge of the lower court as a reason for approaching the judge of the higher court; rather, he pointed to doubt concerning the nullity as a reason for doing so.[41]

In regard to the judge who was delegated for the hearing simply of one particular case, once he had issued his sentence, correctly or incorrectly, his commission was accomplished and his authority and jurisdiction ceased. Therefore such a delegated judge could not reform his sentence if it was vitiated with nullity. In this event it was necessary to approach the superior or the delegating judge. An exception to this procedure was allowed when the sentence was null because of a failure to observe the formalities of the mandate. The reason was that the judge was considered as not having pronounced sentence if he did not observe the formalities of his mandate.[42]

The plaint of nullity when construed as a separate suit could be presented at any time within 30 years. If the plaint of nullity was joined to an appeal, then it had to be utilized within 10 days.[43] In regard to appeals, it was evident that judicial causes committed to a judge with the prohibitive clause which ruled out the benefit of appeal (*appellatione remota*) did not preclude the plaint of nullity.[44]

[40] Engel, lib. II, tit. 28, n. 3; cf. Schmier, lib. II, tract. 3, c. 13, n. 192.

[41] Schmalzgrueber, lib. II, tit. 28, n. 17; cf. Pirhing (1606-1679), *Ius Canonicum in V Libros Decretalium* (ed. novissima, 5 vols., Dilingae, 1722), lib. II, tit. 28, sect. 3, n. 31.

[42] Reiffenstuel, lib. II, tit. 28, n. 30; Pichler, lib. II, tit. 28, n. 5; Engel, lib. II, tit. 28, n. 4.

[43] Pichler, lib. II, tit. 28, n. 5; Pellegrini, pars II, sect. 3, subsect. 2, n. 57; pars III, sect. 1, n. 58; cf. Reiffenstuel, lib. II, tit. 27, n. 137; lib. II, tit. 28, n. 27.

[44] Reiffenstuel, lib. II, tit. 28, nn. 24-25; cf. *supra*, chapter I, n. 3, p. 8.

The exception of nullity was by its very nature perpetual, and could be lodged either before or after the definitive sentence.[45] Moreover, being perpetual by its nature, the exception of nullity could be presented at any time before any competent court.[46]

When the plaint of nullity was invoked against a sentence vitiated with nullity, the execution of that sentence was not impeded unless the nullity was notorious, or manifest from the acts themselves, or could be proved immediately from the acts.[47]

When the plaint of nullity was presented cumulatively with an appeal, Schmier declared that in such instances the execution of the sentence was impeded.[48]

Section 3. More Recent Pre-Code Development

Bouix (1808-1870) declared that the plaint of nullity could be invoked either before the same judge who issued the sentence or before the judge of appeal. To the judge who issued the sentence, the plaint of nullity arising from error was referred, because the error could more easily be corrected by him; to the judge of appeal, the plaint of nullity arising from the malice of the judge of the lower court was presented, because the latter could not readily be expected to acknowledge his malice.[49]

Bouix maintained further that all the doctors preceding him, Reiffensuel, Engel, Pellegrini, and Schmalzgrueber (being attentive to the written law) held to the teaching that the plaint of nullity could be accepted in court either by the judge who had issued the sentence, as long as he acted as an ordinary judge, and not as one delegated simply for the one cause (*ad causam*), or by the appellate judge.[50]

Wernz (1842-1914) maintained that an invalid definitive sen-

[45] Reiffenstuel, lib. II, tit. 25, nn. 45, 70-71; Schmalzgrueber, lib. II, tit. 25, nn. 23-24; Pellegrini, pars III, sect. 1, n. 59.

[46] Reiffenstuel, lib. II, tit. 26, n. 66.

[47] Reiffenstuel, lib. II, tit. 25, 72; lib. II, tit. 28, 26; Engel, lib. II, tit. 28, n. 8; Pichler, lib. II, tit. 28, n. 5.

[48] Schmier, lib. II, tract. 3, c. 13, n. 196.

[49] *Tractatus de Judiciis Ecclesiasticis* (Parisiis, 1855), II, 407-408 (hereafter cited as Bouix).

[50] *Op. cit.*, II, 409.

tence had no juridical force, and that such a sentence could be recalled by the same judge who issued the sentence, provided that he functioned as an ordinary judge. In addition it was not prohibited to propose the plaint of nullity before the superior judge, namely in the court of appeal.[51] Nevertheless, Bouix had stated that at his time the plaint of nullity was lodged only before the judge of appeal in view of the current general custom.[52] The faculty of seeking from the ordinary judge who had issued the sentence a declaration of nullity regarding his own definitive sentence was still acknowledged, even though there was a general custom to the contrary.[53] Wernz quickly added, however, that because of the extant custom that was so widely observed and also in consequence of particular laws, the plaint of nullity not only could but also was to be lodged with the judge of the court that was constituted in law as the court of appeal.[54]

The practice, as mentioned by Wernz and Bouix, of approaching the appellate judge in causes related to the nullity of the sentence was confirmed in some particular laws. Joseph Cardinal Rauscher (1797-1875), Prince-Archbishop of Vienna, drew up and promulgated for his Archdiocese the Austrian Instruction of 1855 in regard to matrimonial causes. This Austrian Instruction declared that the plaint of nullity was to be proposed within the time fixed for appeals before the appellate judge. The sentence thus issued concerning the plaint of nullity precluded all further appeal.[55] Practically the same legislation was found in Cardinal Rauscher's instruction to the tribunal at Prague, wherein it was stated that the plaint of nullity was to be proposed before the judge of appeal within the time set for an appeal, and that the appellate judge's decision in this matter admitted of no further appeal.[56]

[51] *Ius Decretalium*, V, 711.

[52] *Op. cit.*, II, 410.

[53] Wernz, V. 711.

[54] *Op. cit., loc. cit.*

[55] *Instructio Austriaca Josephi Cardinalis Rauscher*, 4 maii, 1855 — *Analecta Iuris Pontificii* (Romae: 1855-1869; Parisiis: 1872-1891), II (1857), 2537-2538.

[56] *Instruction für das Prager fürst-erzbischöfliche Gericht in kirchlichen Angelegenheiten* (1869), §§ 49-59; § 83 — *AKKR*, XXIII (1870), 437-443.

Lega (1860-1935) considered the plaint of nullity as an extraordinary remedy whereby one contended that the sentence which had been issued was null because it labored under a substantial defect. The plaint of nullity could be proposed as a separate suit when the judge who pronounced the sentence was petitioned to declare his own sentence null and void, or as an exception of nullity when the judge was estopped in the execution of the sentence, or the party was estopped in his vindicating of a sentence pronounced in his favor.[57]

Moreover, Lega maintained that the plaint of nullity was to be proposed before the same judge who issued the sentence. He stated that, according to the opinion of the doctors, the plaint of nullity could likewise be proposed to the superior judge, but he refused to accept this procedure and held that, when there was question of a plaint of nullity which was in no way doubtful, then the judge who issued the sentence was to be approached, since less time would thus be consumed and also the expense would be less for the parties.[58]

Bouix offered arguments to substantiate his opinion that the appellate judge alone was to be approached. He refused to accept the opinion that a judge had not completed his office as a result of the nullity that attached to his sentence, and that this same judge should then proceed rightly to judge the same cause again. Bouix reasoned that if the judge issued a first sentence vitiated with nullity, then there acceded also the presumption that he would issue a second null sentence.

Bouix stated that for the purpose of correcting an improper sentence reason itself indicated that the redress should be sought at the hands of the superior judge rather than from him who made the mistake or the error. In regard to him who made the error, it was not unrightfully presumed that he would again commit an error, and thus it was contrary to the public good to approach the same judge who issued the sentence.[59]

[57] *Prelectiones de Iudiciis Civilibus* (2. ed., Romae, 1905, n. 689 (hereafter cited as Lega).

[58] Lega, n. 690.

[59] *Tractatus de Judiciis Ecclesiasticis*, II, 410-411.

The judge who issued the sentence, according to Lega, was to pronounce on the nullity, because even though by pronouncing the sentence the judge had executed his office, and could not further act on his sentence, this procedure held only if the sentence was valid. If the sentence was null, that which was null produced no effect. Moreover, according to the teaching of the jurists, non-existence (*non esse*) and nullity (*esse nullum*) meant the same thing, so that the judge who had issued the sentence could declare its nullity, which made it to be non-existent, and then could proceed anew to issue a sentence. Lega made it clear that he was speaking of an ordinary judge, and not of a judge delegated simply for a particular cause. Such a delegated judge lost his jurisdiction as soon as the sentence was published, and hence he could not act further on his own sentence.[60]

Bouix spoke also of the cumulative appeal, whereby the plaint of nullity was joined together with an appeal in the attacking of an unjust sentence: *Dico sententiam esse nullam; et, si forte talis non sit, appello.*[61]

Lega declared that the cumulative appeal could be used when the sentence was of doubtful nullity. He stated that it was more useful that the one action should not be separated from the other action; and that in the cumulative appeal there was necessitated either a declaration of nullity, or the correction of a valid sentence, or the annulment of the sentence. The cumulative appeal could be made either principally, when the plaint of nullity was joined together with an appeal, or collaterally, when in the course of the trial there was a doubt concerning the nullity of the sentence. The appellate judge, then, was to be approached when the sentence was of doubtful nullity. If the nullity was notorious, however, then not the appellate judge, but only the judge who had issued the sentence, was to be approached.[62]

The plaint of nullity could be proposed throughout a period of 30 years, but not beyond. The reason for this time limit in regard to the entering of a suit was the fact that at the end of

[60] *Op. cit.*, n. 689.
[61] *Op. cit.*, II, 411.
[62] Lega, n. 690; cf. Wernz, V. 711.

this time period the operation of legal prescriptions achieved its full effect.[63]

Bouix declared that a sentence laboring under nullity never became irrevocably adjudged. Following the lead of Pellegrini, Bouix indicated certain exceptions to the operation of the thirty-year prescriptive period for the proposing of the plaint of nullity. The general rule did not apply: (1) if the plaint of nullity was invoked in the nature of a judicial exception, all such exceptions were in their character perpetual; (2) when the sentence was null *ipso iure*, for then the nullity likewise could be regarded as perpetual; (3) when through statutes or by way of customary law a contrary disposition was made in regard to the option of invoking the plaint of nullity; (4) when the nullity of the sentence derived through some defect of jurisdiction or a lack of the needed authorization in regard to the mandate, for then the possible use of the plaint of nullity extended over the period of 1000 years.[64]

In regard to sentences that never became irrevocably adjudged, Lega quoted the opinion of Reiffenstuel to the effect that the plaint of nullity could always be proposed if the nullity had not been sanated by the parties. If the nullity could be sanated by the parties, then the plant of nullity was to be proposed within 10 days, otherwise the parties were considered to have consented to the sentence and sanated it. Lega accepted this opinion, but added that the presumption was a simple one, and would readily yield to contrary proofs.[65]

When the plaint of nullity, as an independent plea in court, was joined cumulatively with an appeal, the plea had to be proposed within 10 days; for in that event it was rather an appeal than a simple plaint of nullity.[66]

In the Papal States, from the time of the sixteenth century, the plea for a *restitutio in integrum* was employed by the Sacred Roman Rota in attacks on the nullity of the sentence.[67] During

[63] Wernz, V. 709; Bouix, II, 411; Lega, p. 691.

[64] Bouix, II, 411.

[65] Lega, pp. 691, 700; Wernz, V, 711.

[66] Lega, p. 691.

[67] Cf. *supra*, Section I of this Chapter, p. 20.

the eighteenth and nineteenth centuries, the Rota continued to employ the plea for a *restitutio in integrum* as the remedy against a null sentence in place of the plaint of nullity.[68]

In 1816, when the judicial system of the Papal States was reformed by Pius VII (1800-1823), he declared that the plea for a *restitutio in integrum* was to be employed against an irrevocably adjudged sentence if some law was neglected or some law was violated in the trial.[69]

In 1834 Gregory XVI (1831-1846) reformed the Papal Courts with his "*Regolamento legislativo e giudicario.*"[70] Gregory declared that any violation of procedural law caused nullity for the judicial act; however, the performance of this act could be repeated if the peremptory limit for the performance of it had not passed. The nullity which derived through a non-substantial defect of form, was to be opposed within three days, otherwise the plaint of nullity was not to be admitted. On the contrary, substantial defects arising from a lack of citation, a deficiency in jurisdiction, or an absence of authorization in the mandate could always be opposed until these defects were waived or sanated.[71]

Gregory XVI further declared that in causes where substantial defects were not sanated or remitted, the plaint of nullity was to be proposed to the appellate court.[72] In regard to a sentence of the Rota that was irrevocably adjudged, he confirmed the use of the plea for a *restitutio in integrum* through a seeking of the redress from the Signatura when there was a neglect of some law or the express contravention of some law in force.[73]

The Rota and the Signatura ceased functioning when the Papal States were in 1870 incorporated into the new Italy. When these tribunals were reinstated by St. Pius X (1903-1914) in

[68] *Cursus Decisiones S.R.R.* (5 vols. in 3, Romae: 1855), dec. 87, n. 1 (June 26, 1822); dec. 299, n. 1 (Feb. 9, 1827); *Decisiones coram Pranetti* (Viterbii, 1839-1840), dec. 176, n. 10 (June 21, 1824).

[69] Motu proprio, "*Reformatio publicae administrationis et tribunalium ditionis Pontificiae,*" 6 iul. 1816, art. 53 — *Bull. Rom. Cont.*, (Prati) XII, 1268.

[70] *Acta Gregorii Papae* (4 vols., Romae, 1901-1904), IV, 300-410.

[71] *Regolamento*, § 408; §§ 778-780.

[72] *Regolamento*, § 789; cf. §§ 977-978.

[73] *Regolamento*, § 1058.

1908, the *Lex Propria* for these tribunals stated that, if the Rotal sentence was confirmatory of another Rotal sentence or the sentence of some other tribunal, then the sentence became irrevocably adjudged and against it no remedy was given except by way of the plaint of nullity or the plea for a *restitutio in integrum*. These remedies were to be invoked before the Apostolic Signatura.[74] The Signatura's competence therefore extended to the plaint of nullity against Rotal sentences. The *Regulae Servandae* of the Signatura in 1912 changed the law of Gregory XVI, so that the neglect of a law or the express violation of some law in force were to be motives for the plaint of nullity and not the *restitutio in integrum*.[75]

When a Rotal sentence was attacked because of nullity, the issue was: "*Sitne nulla rotalis sententia, et sitne locus eius circumscriptioni?*"[76] *Circumscriptio* and the declaration of nullity were two different things. The plaint of nullity could be employed against a sentence vitiated with nullity when the nullity resulted from the omission of the citation, the absence of jurisdiction, or the lack of a mandate, but *circumscriptio* was used if the sentence was otherwise contrary to law or based on an insufficient consideration of the facts.[77]

Finally, in the general law of the Church, the plaint of nullity was explicitly established as the proper remedy against a sentence vitiated with nullity. This remedy was so established by the Code of Canon Law.[78]

[74] *Lex propria, S R. Rotae et Signaturae Ap.*, 29 iun. 1908, can. 33, § 1—*AAS*, I (1909), 29; *Fontes*, n. 6459.

[75] *Lex Propria*, can. 37, § 3 — *AAS*, I (1909), 30; *Fontes*, n. 6459; *Regulae servandae in iudiciis apud Supremum Signaturae Ap. Tribunal*, 6 mart. 1912, art. 4 — *AAS* IV (1912), 189; *Fontes*, n. 6462.

[76] *Lex Propia*, can. 41, § 3 — *AAS*, I (1909), 31; *Fontes*, n. 6459.

[77] Benedictus XV, Chirographum *Attentis expositis*, 28 iun. 1915 (*Appendix ad regulas servandas in iudiciis apud Supremum Signaturae Ap. Tribunal*)—*AAS*, VII (1915), 320-325; *Fontes*, after n. 6462.

[78] Canons 1892-1897.

PART II

CANONICAL COMMENTARY

CHAPTER III

PRELIMINARY NOTIONS

Although no definition of the phrase *querela nullitatis* is found in the Code, the plaint of nullity, as it is understood in canonical legislation, is acknowledged as a remedy against the judicial sentence through a contention in court that the sentence is null because it labors under a substantial defect.[1]

The plaint of nullity is considered as a remedy, just as is the appeal and the plea for a *restitutio in integrum*. Remedies of law are defined as the legally acknowledged means by which parties can defend themselves against processual injury caused in consequence of some decree issued in court, or of some omission of a requisite in the trial, or in general as the result of some disallowed action or omission.[2] These remedies are divided into ordinary and extraordinary remedies. The ordinary remedy can be distinguished from an extraordinary remedy either by the condition of the persons to whom it is granted or by the time which the use of the remedy is permitted.[3] Cocchi made a simple distinction between ordinary and extraordinary remedies. He stated that an ordinary remedy proceeds from the general principles of law, whereas an extraordinary remedy proceeds from a derogation of the general principles of the law.[4] There are some authors[5]

[1] Noval, *Commentarium Codicis Iuris Canonici*, Lib. IV, *De Processibus*, Pars. I, *De Iudiciis* (Augustae Taurinorum — Romae, 1920), n. 657 (hereafter cited *De Iudiciis*); Coronata, *Institutiones Iuris Canonici* (5 vols., Taurini: Marietti, Vol. III, 3. ed., 1948), n. 1417; Wernz-Vidal, *Ius Canonicum*, VI, n. 614.

[2] Vermeersch-Creusen, *Epitome Iuris Canonici* (6. ed., 3 vols., Mechliniae-Romae: Dessain, 1937-1946), III (1946), n. 235 (hereafter this work will be referred to as *Epitome*).

[3] Cf. canons 1881; 1883; 1893; 1895; 1905.

[4] Canon 1905.

[5] Lega, *Commentarius in Iudicia Ecclesiastica iuxta Codicem Iuris Canonici* (3 vols., Romae: Anonima Libraria Cattolica Italiana, ed. V. Bartoccetti,

who maintain that the plaint of nullity is an extraordinary remedy. It hardly appears that it could now be so called, since the plaint of nullity has entered the list of ordinary remedies of redress as stated in Canon 1905.

The plaint of nullity against the sentence differs intrinsically from the appeal in that it is interposed because of a defect extrinsic to the sentence, a defect of form, while, on the contrary, the appeal is lodged because of an intrinsic defect in the sentence, namely for the reason that the sentence is unjust or does not conform to the rights of the parties.[6] The defect spoken of here is extrinsic to the sentence and must be a substantial defect in order that the plaint of nullity may be employed for the purpose of attacking the nullity of the sentence. The Code makes it definite when it declares that for an act to be null and void there must be wanting either the essential constituents of the act, or some formalities or conditions which the Code requires under pain of nullity.[7] These defects, in so far as the plaint of nullity is concerned, must be of a substantial nature as defined by law. Such substantial defects which cannot be rectified are the following: a sentence which has been pronounced by a judge who was absolutely incompetent to render a decision;[8] a sentence issued by a collegiate tribunal consisting of an insufficient number of judges;[9] a sentence that has been issued to parties of whom one had no right to stand in court,[10] and a sentence that was given

1938-1941, Vol. I (1950), II (1939), n. 2, p. 1015 (hereafter this work will be referred to as *Commentarius*); Lemieux, *The Sentence in Ecclesiastical Procedure*, The Catholic University of America Canon Law Studies, n. 87 (Washington, D.C.: The Catholic University of America, 1934), p. 92; Kealy, *The Introductory Libellus in Church Court Procedure*, The Catholic University of America Canon Law Studies, n. 108 (Washington, D.C.: The Catholic University of America, 1937), p. 67; Hogan, *Judicial Advocates and Procuratores*, The Catholic University of America Canon Law Studies, n. 133 (Washington, D.C.: The Catholic University of America Press, 1941), p. 168.

[6] Coronata, *Institutiones Iuris Canonici*, III, n. 1417; Wernz-Vidal, *Ius Canonicum*, VI, n. 614.

[7] Canon 1680, § 1.

[8] Cf. canons 1556-1558; 1892, 1°.

[9] Cf. canons 1576, § 1; 1892, 1°.

[10] Cf. canons 1646-1654; 1892, 2°.

in a case in which somebody acted in the name of another without a legitimate mandate;[11]

Substantial defects which can be rectified are the following: a sentence that is issued in a case wherein the legitimate summons was omitted;[12] a sentence in which the motives or reasons for the decision are lacking;[13] a sentence that does not contain all the personal signatures which the law demands,[14] and, finally, a sentence that does not bear a notation of the year, the month, the day, and the place of its issue.[15]

Whether the enumerations of the defects mentioned in canons 1892 and 1894 are all-inclusive or merely demonstrative will be the subject matter of a later chapter.[16] Doheny declares that a plaint of nullity is a formal allegation of an aggrieved party addressed to the court issuing the sentence against some extrinsic defect, such as some irregularity or error, of the sentence, while an appeal is a formal request of an aggrieved party to a higher court against some intrinsic element, such as the alleged inherent injustice of a sentence rendered by a lower tribunal. Consequently, if but one individual as judge conducted a matrimonial trial and issued a sentence, the legal remedy of a plaint of nullity could be lodged against such a sentence. An appeal, however, is directed against the alleged injustice of the sentence, or the hardship wrought by it upon the party or parties to whom it has been unfavorable.[17] Lega stated that the substantial difference between the plaint of nullity and the appeal is that the plaint of nullity is presented before the same judge who issued the sentence, whereas the appeal is made to a higher judge.[18] This does not seem correct, for the history of the plaint of nullity clearly

[11] Cf. canons 1659; 1660; 1892, 3°.

[12] Cf. canons 1723; 1711, § 2; 1894, 1°.

[13] Cf. canons 1873, § 1, 3°; 1894, 2°.

[14] Cf. canons 1874, § 5; 1894, 3°.

[15] Cf. canons 201, § 2; 1637; 1874, § 5; 1894, 4°.

[16] Cf. Chapter VII.

[17] *Canonical Procedure in Matrimonial Cases*, Vol. I, *Formal Judicial Procedure* (2. ed. Milwaukee: Bruce Publishing Co., 1948), p. 510 (hereafter cited *Canonical Procedure*).

[18] *Commentarius*, II, 1015.

indicates that the plaint of nullity was also lodged before the appellate judge, and likewise canon 1895 permits the plaint of nullity to be joined cumulatively with an appeal in certain cases. In this regard, however, care must be taken that the plaint of nullity be combined with the allegation of injustice as an accessory motive, and not as the principal reason for the appeal; otherwise, the appeal will not be admitted.[19] Moreover, the plaint of nullity as an exception may be proposed before any tribunal.[20]

The plaint of nullity also differs substantially from the plea for a *restitutio in integrum*,[21] which is an extraordinary remedy of the law by which a person who has been gravely damaged by a valid but rescissible act or transaction may, because of natural equity, be returned, through the ministry of a competent judge, to that status in which he was before being damaged.[22] Since the plea for a *restitutio in integrum* is an extraordinary remedy, it can be employed only when no other action or remedy, e.g., an appeal or a plaint of nullity, is possible.[23]

A sentence which is null must never be confused with a sentence that does not exist. A sentence is said not to exist when it does not proceed from judicial authority, or if it does not have the semblance of a sentence, e.g., if the sentence is issued by one who is not a judge, or if only the private conclusions of the judges are presented. In these cases it is enough to examine the specious sentence to see that it is not a true sentence. No special action is required to attack its validity.[24]

A sentence which is null, however, is one which is legitimately issued by the judge and has the semblance of a true sentence,

[19] Connolly, *Appeals*, The Catholic University of America Canon Law Studies, n. 79 (The Catholic University of America, 1932), p. 76.

[20] Cf. canon 1667; Reiffenstuel, lib. II, tit. 26, n. 66; Coronata, *Institutiones Iuris Canonici*, III, n. 1419; Vermeersch-Creusen, *Epitome*, III, n. 242.

[21] Cf. canons 1687-1689; 1905-1907.

[22] Feeney, *Restitutio in Integrum*, The Catholic University of America Canon Law Studies, n. 129 (Washington, D.C.: The Catholic University of America Press, 1941), pp. 49-50; Reiffenstuel, lib. I, tit. 41, n. 3.

[23] Feeney, *op. cit.*, p. 51.

[24] Roberti, *De Processibus*, II, n. 487; Cappello, *Summa Iuris Canonici*, Vol. III (editio altera emendata et aucta, Romae: Apud aedes Universitatis Gregorianae, 1940), n. 268.

but labors under some defect, so that it cannot be upheld.[25] Against such a sentence a plaint of nullity can be duly proposed.

The nullity of a sentence may be remediable or irremediable. Lega stated that the basis of this distinction is to be found in the fact that remediable nullity rests upon those reasons which directly concern the private advantage of the parties, and thus may be renounced or waived by the parties, either expressly, or tacitly by not using the remedy within the time limit, while, on the other hand, irremediable nullity rests upon reasons which concern the public good, and therefore cannot be renounced by private individuals.[26] Roberti states that the distinction between the two classes lies in the difference of the time period in which, in line with the differing gravity of the judicial causes, the suit of nullity reaches its conclusion.[27] Noone is of the opinion that both views are correct. He declares further that Lega's opinion states more incisively the essential difference between the two causes of nullity, and that it is more in harmony with the liberal meaning of the terms remediable and irremediable.[28] Roberti's opinion, however, seems to disregard completely the plaint of nullity as an exception,[29] for he declares that the distinction between remediable and irremediable nullity looks simply to a difference of the time period in which the suit (*actio*) of nullity reaches its conclusion. This matter will be discussed in detail in a later chapter.[30]

Nullity, therefore, is remediable if a solemnity required in the law for validity is omitted, namely: when the legal summons is

[25] Roberti, *loc. cit.*,; Cappello, *loc. cit.*

[26] *Commentarius*, II, 1015; Wernz-Vidal, *Ius Canonicum*, VI, n. 614; Vermeersch-Creusen, *Epitome*, III, n. 241.

[27] *De Processibus*, II, n. 488; Cappello states: ". . . quae assertio, ut patet, rationem veri fundamenti iuridici non assignat." — *Summa Iuris Canonicis*, III, n. 269 (hereafter cited *Summa*).

[28] Noone, *Nullity in Judicial Acts*, The Catholic University of America Canon Law Studies, n. 297 (Washington, D.C.: The Catholic University of America Press, 1950), p. 102.

[29] Coyle, *Judicial Exceptions*, The Catholic University of America Canon Law Studies, n. 193 (Washington, D.C.: The Catholic University of America Press, 1944), p. 55.

[30] Cf. Article 1 of Chapter VI.

lacking; when the motives for the decision are not made part of the wording of the sentence; when the required signatures are lacking; and when all or even any of the indications of the day, the month, the year, and the place in which the sentence was given are missing.[31]

Irremediable nullity arises when the sentence has been issued by a judge who is absolutely incompetent, or in a collegiate trial by an insufficient number of judges; when at least one of the parties lacks the right to stand in judgment; and when a procurator lacks the legitimate mandate which the law requires as essential.[32]

[31] Canon 1894; Vermeersch-Creusen, *Epitome,* III, n. 241.
[32] Canon 1892.

CHAPTER IV

IRREMEDIABLE NULLITY OF THE SENTENCE

Canon 1892. *Sententia vitio insanabilis nullitatis laborat quando:*

1°. Lata est a iudice absolute incompetente vel in tribunali collegiali a non legitimo iudicum numero contra praescriptum can. 1576, §1;

2°. Lata est inter partes, quarum altera saltem non habet personam standi in iudicio;

3°. Quis nomine alterius egit sine legitimo mandato.

As is evident from canon 1892, an irremediable nullity is a defect of the sentence which is of a serious nature, and one that originates not from the sentence but rather from certain defects extrinsic to the sentence.

Article 1. Absolute Incompetence

Canon 1892. *Sententia vitio insanabilis nullitatis laborat quando: 1°. Lata est a iudica absolute incompetente.*

Competence in general is defined as judicial jurisdiction which is commensurate with and limited to certain causes and persons. It is simply jurisdiction considered in the concrete.[1] In other words, competence is that definite jurisdiction by which a certain tribunal is empowered to judge a specific cause of certain individuals in a determined territory. Not all tribunals can settle all controversies indiscriminately. The nature of the causes, the persons involved, and the territorial extent of the jurisdiction must be taken into consideration. It is for this reason that a diocesan tribunal can adjudge only those causes that are subject to its jurisdiction according to the rulings of Canon Law.[2]

Incompetence, then, is the lack of jurisdiction in a judge with reference to a certain cause or controversy which is submitted

[1] Coronata, *Institutiones Iuris Canonici*, III, n. 1093; Wernz-Vidal, *Ius Canonicum*, VI, n. 46; Vermeersch-Creusen, *Epitome*, III, n. 10; Reiffenstuel, lib. II, tit, 2, nn. 3-4; Pichler, lib. II, tit. 2, nn. 2-3.

[2] Doheny, *Canonical Procedure*, I, 14-15; Noval, *De Iudiciis* n. 58.

to him.[3] Judicial incompetence is either absolute or relative. It is absolute if a cause is completely taken away from the jurisdiction of a judge. Such incompetency obtains in a subordinate judge in relation to causes reserved[4] or legitimately called to a higher tribunal.[5] Relative incompetence is present when the judge, though he may possess jurisdiction, does not have a legally recognized title on which to decide the particular cause which is submitted to him.[6]

Absolute incompetence has its source in the principles of public law, so that the judicial order constituted for the public good will be observed. Absolute incompetence can in no manner be made good. Relative incompetence flows from the law defending private rights, and is that by which a judge is incompetent in relation to a particular cause.[7]

A judge or tribunal may be absolutely incompetent because of the dignity of the parties involved in the cause. The Primatial See can be judged by no one.[8] The Supreme Pontiff has the highest legislative, administrative, and judicial power in the Church, and, therefore, he can be judged by no power on earth. No one can be judged by another to whose jurisdiction he is not subject; and in the Church there is no person, either physical or moral, to whom the Roman Pontiff is subject. Moreover, the Supreme Pontiff is the font, as it were, whence is derived all jurisdiction over the members of the Church. Since this is true, only

[3] Wernz-Vidal, *Ius Canonicum*, VI, n. 47; Noval, *loc. cit.*

[4] Cf. canons 1556-1557, §§ 1, 2.

[5] Cf. canon 1557, § 3.

[6] Cf. canons 1560-1568; Lega, *Commentarius*, I (1950), 38; Wernz-Vidal, *Ius Canonicum*, VI, n. 47.

[7] Cf. canons 1560-1568; Burke, *Competence in Ecclesiastical Tribunals*, The Catholic University of America, Canon Law Studies, n. 14 (Washington, D.C.: The Catholic University of America, 1922), p. 14; Wernz-Vidal, *Ius Canonicum*, VI, n. 47.

[8] Canon 1556. Canon 100, § 1: "Catholica Ecclesia et Apostolica Sedes moralis personae rationem habent ex ipsa ordinatione divina." The distinction between the Catholic Church and the Apostolic See is a real, though unequal distinction, i.e., one is part of the other. The Apostolic See, in this meaning, does not include the departments of the Roman Curia. — Coronata, *Institutiones Iuris Canonici*, I, n. 138bis.

the Supreme Pontiff is immune from all human judgment.[9]

Although the term Apostolic See or Holy See, wherever it occurs in the Code, means not only the Roman Pontiff but also, unless the context indicates the contrary, the Sacred Congregations and the Roman Tribunals and Offices through which the Roman Pontiff usually transacts the affairs of the Universal Church,[10] the law that the Primatial See can be judged by no one must be understood as referring to the Roman Pontiff (as the visible Head of the Church), because of the meaning of the law and also because of the importance of the matter involved. All persons, therefore, who help the Supreme Pontiff to govern the Church, as found in the various Roman Congregations, Tribunals, and Offices, can be judged in trial, and, consequently, are excluded from the term "Primatial See" in canon 1556.[11]

All ecclesiastical judges, with the exception of the Supreme Pontiff, are absolutely incompetent to judge the causes of those

[9] Wernz-Vidal, *Ius Canonicum*, VI, n. 49; Coronata, *Institutiones Iuris Canonici*, III, n. 1095; Vermeersch-Creusen, *Epitome*, III, n. 11. The judicial immunity of the pope from all temporal jurisdiction follows as a corollary from the reverence and the respect due to the Vicar of Christ on earth. More basically, it is one of those essential means, and necessary liberties, which are proper, natural, and inalienable to the Church in its capacity of a juridically perfect society. Without it, the divine mission of the Church would be neither secure, since it would continue subject to abusive and hostile interference from temporal magistrates, nor stable, inasmuch as it would be affected by political turbulence and revolution, nor acceptable to all the peoples of the world, for the reason that it could constantly be suspected as a tool for the furtherance of the political ambitions of politicians. It would entail the perversion of the divine order of things, making the spiritual subject to the material, the eternal to the temporal, the sacred to the profane. Papal immunity is, therefore, rooted in the natural divine law, and draws at least an implicit corroboration from the positive divine law. — Bourque, *The Judicial Power of the Church*, The Catholic University of America Canon Law Studies, n. 337 (The Catholic University of America Press, 1953), pp. 129-130; cf. Coronata, *Ius Publicum Ecclesiasticum* (3. ed., Romae: Marietti, 1948), nn. 156-8; Ottaviani, *Institutione Iuris Publici Ecclesiastici* (3, ed., 2 vols., Civitate Vaticana: Typis Polyglottis Vaticanis, 1947), I, 217.

[10] Canon 7.

[11] Roberti, *De Processibus*, I, (2. ed.) n. 63; Wernz-Vidal, *Ius Canonicum*, VI, n. 49; Lega, *Commentarius*, I (1950) 32.

who hold the highest governmental rank in a nation.[12] This would include the king or queen of a country, or some other personage who would come under this title of Chief of State. In a democratic state, the president of the country, and in the United States of America the governors of States would be included because they are the actual rulers of the individual States. The exclusive right to judge the causes of the sons and daughters of these rulers also pertains to the Roman Pontiff, as does the right to judge those who have the immediate right of succession. The immediate right of succession, however, must be a right (*ius*) and not merely a hope of succeeding to the government. Those who have this right of immediate succession to the supreme government of a people would include heirs-apparent, vice-presidents, presidents-elect, lieutenant-governors of the States in the United States whenever they have the right of immediate succession, and governors-elect of the States of the United States.[13] The wives of the above-mentioned rulers, though not expressly named in the Code, are nevertheless included implicitly among the persons subject to this special forum.[14]

The Roman Pontiff has the exclusive right to judge the cases of Cardinals from the day of their promotion in consistory to the cardinalitial rank.[15] All other ecclesiastical judges are absolutely incompetent since Cardinals, after the Roman Pontiff, are the highest ecclesiastical dignitaries and are called *partes sui corporis* by the Supreme Pontiff because of their excellence of honor and

[12] Canon 1557, § 1, 1°.

[13] Canons 1557, § 1, 1°; 1558; Roberti, *De Processibus*, I, (2. ed.) n. 63; Noval, *De Iudiciis*, n. 64; Doheny, *Canonical Procedure*, I, 512-513; Coronata, *Institutiones Iuris Canonici*, III, n. 1096; Wernz-Vidal, *Ius Canonicum*, VI, Lega, *Commentarius*, I, (1950) 33.

[14] Canon 1112; Roberti states: Uxores . . . comprehenduntur sive quia matrimonio statum assequuntur mariti sive a pari immo a fortiori a filiabus argumento deducto. — *De Processibus*, I, (2. ed.) n. 63; Wernz-Vidal declare: Coniuges . . . videntur implicite contineri . . . tum ex eadem convenientia sociali et participatione specialis honoris, tum ex hoc quod rex et regina habentur ad modum unius personae. — *Ius Canonicum*, VI, n. 49; Cf. Lega, *Commentarius*, I, 35.

[15] Canon 1557, § 1, 2°; Roberti, *De Processibus*, I, (2. ed.) n. 63; cf. canons 233; 239, § 1; 1600; 2227.

dignity.[16]

All judges subordinate to the Roman Pontiff cannot hear and decide the causes of legates of the Apostolic See as long as these legates remain in office. As a result these judges are absolutely incompetent with regard to the causes of legates *a latere*, of nuncios, or internuncios, and of apostolic delegates. Not reserved to the Roman Pontiff are the causes of those who possess merely the honorific title of apostolic legate.[17] Finally these judges are absolutely incompetent in regard to criminal causes of bishops, even titular bishops.[18]

It is not necessary in all the causes reserved to the Roman Pontiff by canon 1557, §1, that the Supreme Pontiff himself judge these causes; he is wont to delegate the hearing of such causes to one of the Sacred Congregations or to a commission of Cardinals.[19]

Because of the dignity of the parties involved, judges or tribunals likewise are absolutely incompetent in all causes which are reserved to the tribunals of the Holy See. The contentious causes of residential bishops can be judged only by the tribunals of the Holy See, with the exception of causes which concern the temporal rights or goods of the bishop, or of the episcopal *mensa*, or of the diocesan curia, or of other moral persons that the bishop might represent. Those excepted causes can be referred, with the consent of the bishop, to a collegiate tribunal of his own diocese, or carried to the judge of the immediately higher court.[20]

In view of canon 1572, §2,[21] the question naturally arises concerning just what contentious causes are reserved to the tribunals

[16] Canon 1558; Wernz-Vidal, *Ius Canonicum*, VI, n. 49; Lega, *Commentarius*, I, (1950) 35.

[17] Canons 1557, § 1, 3°; 1558; 266; 267; 270; 1600; 2227; Roberti, *De Processibus*, I, n. 63; Lega, *Commentarius*, I, 35.

[18] Canons 1557, § 1, 3°; 1558; 2227; cf. Wernz-Vidal, *Ius Canonicum*, VI, n. 49.

[19] Roberty, *De Processibus*, I, n. 63; cf. canon 1962.

[20] Canons 1557, § 2, 1°; 1572, § 2; 1653, § 5.

[21] Canon 1572, § 2. Si vero agatur de iuribus aut bonis temporalibus Episcopi aut mensae vel Curiae dioecesanae, controversia dirimenda deferatur vel, Episcopo consentiente, ad dioecesanum tribunal collegiale quod constat officiali et duobus iudicibus synodalibus antiquioribus, vel ad iudicem immediate superiorem.

of the Holy See. Lega stated that all contentious causes of residential bishops *de statu personae* are reserved to the tribunals of the Holy See. By the expression, *de statu personae,* he implied such questions as are concerned with the personal status of the bishop, e.g., whether or not the bishop is legitimate by birth.[22] Cappello declares that only private causes concerning residential bishops are reserved.[23] McElroy believes that neither of these authors is clear in his treatment of the problem concerning the litigated temporal rights and goods of a bishop. He offers his own explanation, which is based on a distinction that the Sacred Roman Rota considered between the bishop as a subject of rights and property and the bishop as a private person. When the cause is primarily concerned with the rights and property of the bishop and only secondarily with the bishop himself, the ruling of canon 1572, §2, is to be followed. The trial, then, may be held before a collegiate tribunal of the diocese or the judges of the immediately superior court. When the case is primarily concerned with the bishop and only secondarily with the bishop's rights and property, canon 1557, §2, 1°, is to be followed. The trial in this latter event is to be held before the Rota. McElroy admits, however, that the Rota did not clearly explain the relationship existing between canon 1557, §2, 1°, and canon 1572, §2, when it made the distinction which he uses as the basis for his opinion. He further declares that there are many causes in which it would be difficult to make such a distinction.[24]

To the writer it seems that a different distinction should be made for the proper understanding of these canons. By a contentious trial is meant a civil trial dealing with disputed rights and claims, as well as damage caused by negligence, etc. In civil suits private persons, either physical or moral, implore the protection of the courts against other persons who impugn their rights and claims.[25]

[22] *Commentarius,* I, 36.

[23] *Summa,* III, n. 14.

[24] *The Privileges of Bishops,* The Catholic University of America Canon Law Studies, n. 282 (Washington, D.C.: The Catholic University of America Press, 1951), pp. 105-106.

[25] Cf. Woywod, "Procedural Law of the Church," *The Homiletic and Pastoral Review* (New York, 1900-), XXX (1930), 729.

By reason of its object, right is divided into a *ius in re* and a *ius ad rem.* A *ius in re* connotes a situation in which a person has a thing attaching to himself in such a manner that he has an immediate power over the thing. On that basis there is room for a real action in relation to the object and there exists a rightful capacity for demanding this thing wherever it may be found. It is, therefore, a right as against all the world to claim title to a specific thing.[26]

A *ius ad rem* is that right which one or more individuals have against one or more other individuals in order that a thing may become his or their own. There is no question of a real action in relation to the object, nor is there given any right of immediately disposing of the object. All that a *ius ad rem* grants is a personal action against the one who is holding the thing in question.[27]

There are certain conditions required for a *ius in re.* There must be some particular thing in existence and it must have been acquired by some lawful title.[28] If, however, any of these conditions is wanting, then there is question not of a *ius in re*, but simply of a *ius ad rem*, for which one condition suffices, namely a just and lawful title. In the case of a *ius in re* there is question of actual dominion, and not necessarily of physical possession. If a party own an automobile and loses physical possession of it by theft, he still retains this right, i.e., the *ius in re.* Moreover, if

[26] Merkelbach, *Summa Theologiae Moralis*, Vol. II (5. ed., Parisiis, 1947), n. 158: "Ius in re est illud quod quis habet in re iam sua et obtenta, unde dat actionem realem in ipsam rem, et facultatem legitimam disponendi de ipsa re, ac illam sibi vindicandi ubicumque sit et a quocumque detineatur."

[27] Merkelbach, *loc. cit.*: "Ius ad rem est illud quod quis habet ut res aliqua fiat sua, unde non dat actionem in ipsam rem, nec facultatem disponendi immediate de re, sed actionem in personam debitoris tantum ad rem obtinendam."

[28] Ad ius in re tres requiruntur conditiones:

1) ut res revera existat, secus non potest hic et nunc devinciri in proprium commodum;

2) ut in individuo sit debita, secus nullum determinatum vinculum cum ea esse potest;

3) ut alicui devinciatur titulo legitimo vi cuius dicere hic et nunc possit: haec res est mea. — Merkelbach, *op. cit., loc. cit.*

someone takes something over which another person has actual dominion, the latter person has the right to take it back (real action) in any way he pleases. On the other hand, a *ius ad rem* confers a personal right, i.e., a right to acquire actual dominion. If a party makes a contract to buy something and refuses to execute the purchase from the seller, then the latter party can enter a personal suit against the prospective buyer.[29]

With this in mind, the writer offers the following explanations for the proper understanding of the relationship of canon 1572, §2, to canon 1557, §2, 1°. Under the name of temporal rights and goods of the bishop are understood all those things which are the object of contentious suits or actions at law — all real claims of actions at law which concern the rights which the bishop has over lands and goods, and all personal judicial claims or actions which are directed against persons themselves with the view to obtaining some temporal thing. When the cause is concerned with these real and personal judicial claims or actions, the ruling of canon 1572, §2, 1°, is to be observed. The trial in such causes is held before a tribunal of three judges of the diocese, or carried to the proper superior court. For example, if there is question of the bishop's right to a piece of property, or if the bishop is involved in a cause on the basis of his failure to fulfill a contract, or his failure to pay a debt, such causes are to be tried in the diocesan tribunal.

Opposed to the temporal rights and goods of the bishop, the prosecution and vindication of which are subject to a collegiate tribunal,[30] are those rights which arise from the *status* of the person. The writer agrees with Lega in his statement that by the expression, *de statu personae*, one is to understand such questions as are concerned with the personal status of the bishop, e.g., whether or not the bishop is legitimate by birth.[31] Such causes are reserved to the Rota.[32]

In a word, the ruling of canon 1572, §2, does not pertain to the

[29] Cf. Merkelbach, *op. cit.*, *loc. cit.*

[30] Cf. canon 1572, § 2.

[31] Cf. Lega, *Commentarius*, 1, (1950) 36.

[32] Cf. canon 1557, § 2, 1°.

person of a bishop or to his diocese, but only to causes which can be called fiscal (*fiscales*).[33]

There can be no doubt that contentious causes which involve the temporal rights and goods of the bishop's benefice (*mensa episcopalis*), and also of the diocesan curia, may be judged in a collegiate diocesan tribunal with the consent of the bishop. Canon 1557, §2, 1°, does not reserve these causes to the tribunals of the Holy See.[34]

In addition to the residential bishops, titular bishops when acting as Apostolic Administrators, and also coadjutors of totally disabled bishops, enjoy the favor of this reservation of canon 1557, §2, 1° because they function as a ruler in a diocese.[35] Abbots and prelates *nullius*, and also vicars and prefects apostolic are considered as equal to bishops in this reservation. Titular bishops as such, however, do not enjoy this reservation with reference to contentious causes, but are subject to local tribunals.[36]

All judges of tribunals subordinate to the tribunals of the Holy See are absolutely incompetent to judge the causes of dioceses and other ecclesiastical legal persons who have no superior below the Supreme Pontiff, such as exempt religious of either solemn or simple vows who have been withdrawn from the jurisdiction of the local ordinary, and monastic congregations.[37] The causes here reserved are those that concern moral persons as such, and not the individual members who belong to these collegiate institutes. Therefore, individual houses or provinces of religious institutes are not included, for they have ordinary superiors who are competent to try their causes.[38]

In considering the causes reserved to the Roman Pontiff or to the tribunals of the Holy See, Roberti maintains that these reservations are in force only when the parties mentioned in canon

[33] Cf. Beste, *Introductio in Codicem* (3. ed., Collegeville, Minn.: St. John's Abbey Press, 1946), p. 783.

[34] Roberti, *De Processibus*, I, (2. ed.) n. 97.

[35] Cappello, *Summa*, III, n. 27; Roberti, *De Processibus*, I, (2. ed.) n. 63.

[36] Roberti, *loc. cit.*; Coronata, *Institutiones Iuris Canonici*, III, n. 1097; canons 215, § 2; 249. § 1.

[37] Canons 1557, § 2, 2°; 1558.

[38] Lega, *Commentarius*, I, 37 and 137; cf. canons 99; 100; 488, 8°.

1557 are defendants in the trial in accordance with the principle "*actor sequitur forum rei.*"[39] Noone states that this interpretation by Roberti seems hardly tenable, for at least in part it would defeat the purpose of the reservation. If a cause were not reserved when a high-ranking personage acts in the capacity of plaintiff, such a plaintiff could unduly use his position for influencing the judges of the lower tribunal to the detriment of the defendant.[40]

The writer holds the latter opinion for several reasons. The principle, "the plaintiff must follow the forum of the defendant,"[41] by its very position in the Code of Canon Law, is concerned with the question of relative competence which follows canon 1559, and accordingly it should not be considered applicable to the preceding canons which deal with the reservation of causes to the Holy See. Moreover, this privilege of a special forum according to its terms comprehends the entire trial, and does not make a distinction between the plaintiff and the defendant. Furthermore, the plaintiff, too, is subject to the jurisdiction of the court. Before a judge admits a plaintiff to plead his cause, he is bound to ascertain whether the plaintiff has a right in law to sue.[42]

The Code also declares that if a judge cannot attain moral certainty about the matter which is to be defined by the sentence,[43] he shall announce that the right of the plaintiff has not been established, and he shall discharge the defendant.[44] Besides, an irrevocable sentence[45] makes law for the parties and bars further

[39] Roberti, *De Processibus*, I, n. 63.

[40] Noone, *Nullity in Judicial Acts*, p. 29.

[41] Canon 1559, § 3.

[42] Cf. canon 1609, §2.

[43] Canon 1868, § 1: "A judicial sentence is a legitimate pronouncement by which the judge decides a cause proposed by the litigants and tried in judicial form; the sentence is interlocutory, if it decides an incidental cause; definitive, if it settles the principal cause."

[44] Cf. canon 1869, § 4. If there is question of a so-called *causa favorabilis*, e.g., of a matrimonial cause with reference to the validity of the marriage, then the sentence must be rendered in favor of the validity when the matter remains doubtful; in a cause concerning the right of possession, the parties are to be given joint possession, if the judge remains doubtful.

[45] Cf. canon 1902.

proceedings if one of the parties attempts to bring the other party to court on the same matter.[46] It must be noted that a judicial sentence creates rights and obligations between the parties; in fact, a judicial sentence determines the rights between the parties engaged in litigation.[47] With the foregoing arguments in mind, the writer holds the view that the parties mentioned in canon 1557, either as plaintiffs or as defendants, are subject to the exclusive judgment of the Roman Pontiff or of one of the tribunals of the Apostolic See.

Other causes which the Roman Pontiff has called to his tribunal shall be adjudicated by the judge whom the Supreme Pontiff himself appoints. Because of his immediate jurisdiction over all the faithful, clergy and laity alike, the Roman Pontiff can take cognizance of a cause, whether in character it be contentious or criminal, at any stage whatsoever of the procedure. He can do this on his own motion or at the request of a party involved. Therefore, if he does so, all other judges are absolutely incompetent.[48]

An ecclesiastical judge or tribunal may also be absolutely incompetent because of the object or the subject-matter of a cause. The Congregation of the Holy Office has exclusive jurisdiction in causes which involve the Pauline Privilege. Any other tribunal would be absolutely incompetent.[49]

Absolute incompetence may according to the doctrine of some authors arise also through a consideration of the element relating to the instance in which the cause is being heard or prosecuted.[50] It is for the reason that a cause is being prosecuted in higher instance that a court of appeal becomes competent. In view of the fact that the court of second instance is the legally established appellate tribunal for a particular court of first instance, it thereby possesses the necessary jurisdiction to hear causes properly ap-

[46] Cf. canon 1904, § 2.

[47] Cf. canon 17, § 3.

[48] Canons 1557, § 3; 1569, § 1; 1558; cf. Roberti, *De Processibus*, I, (2. ed.) n. 63; Lega, *Commentarius*, I, (1950) 38.

[49] Cf. canons 247, § 3; 1962.

[50] Cf. Burke, *Competence in Ecclesiastical Tribunals*, p. 14; Wernz-Vidal, *Ius Canonicum*, VI, n. 47; Noval, *De Iudiciis*, I, n. 60.

pealed from that court. This type of competence is not explicitly stated in the Code, but it is, according to Lane, implied in a number of canons of the Code.[51]

The lack of competence arising in consequence of the instance in which the cause is being presented is something absolute. The various tribunals are for their valid judicial activity restricted to the hearing of any cause in some specifically indicated instance of the trial. According to the Pontifical Commission for the Authentic Interpretation of the Code,[52] a cause once heard in the court of first instance cannot be heard again by any tribunal in the same instance; it can be heard, but only in a superior court after an appeal has been filed.

Roberti considers his competence under the title of "*competentia functionalis.*" Such competence has special application for the various grades of jurisdiction execised in the divers instances within a trial.[53]

[51] Canons 1572, § 1; 1594; 1599, § 1, 1°; 1879-1891, § 1; cf. Lane, *Matrimonial Procedure in the Ordinary Courts of Second Instance*, The Catholic University of America Canon Law Studies, n. 253 (Washington, D.C.: The Catholic University of America Press, 1947), p. 59.

[52] Pont. Comm., Interp., resp. 16 iun. 1931 — *AAS*, XXIII (1931), 353.

[53] Roberti extends functional competence to include not only the appellate instance of the trial, but also the remedies of law against the sentence and the execution of the sentence. He declares: "De competentia autem functionali, quem doctores moderni in Germani atque in Italia recentiore tempore introduxerunt ut eadem comprehenderent nedum varias instantias iudiciales, sed omnes activitates circa eandem causam a diversis tribunalibus exercendas, usque adhuc loqui canonistae praetermiserunt. Quin immo ipsa Codicis schemata haud magnam lucem afferunt huic questioni, cum tantum initio loquantur de competentia ratione gradus et postea videantur, specie saltem, hanc ipsam praetermisisse. Codex ipse de hoc competentiae capite sub titulo de foro competenti minime loquitur.

Existentia competentiae functionalis nihilominus in Codice ferit oculos. Eadem comprehendit praesertim gradus iurisdictionis, remedia iuris contra sententiam et sententiae executionem nec non aliquot alios casus." — *De Processibus*, I, (2. ed.) n. 62. Noone agrees with Roberti and seeks to prove that absolute incompetence is involved when judges or tribunals other than those mentioned in the law attempt performance of these judicial functions.— *Nullity in Judicial Acts*, pp. 30-32. Instead, however, of the question of absolute incompetence, it seems to the writer that canon 1680, §1, is involved. This canon states: "An act is null and void only when there are wanting the

Noone states that judicial nullity may arise because of a deficiency in the delegated jurisdiction of a judge. He says that this deficiency may be in the delegating authority, or in the delegate; or it may arise because the delegate exceeds the terms of his mandate, or because of the expiration of his mandate.[54] The writer agrees with Noone when he declares that the acts of a delegated judge, when his jurisdiction has expired in any of the foregoing ways, have no value in the external ecclesiastical forum. The writer, however, disagrees with Noone when the latter tries to earmark these causes as having been presented with absolute incompetence, so that they become affected with an irremediable nullity.[55] It seems to the writer that when canon 1680, §1, declares acts to be null and void if essential constituents are lacking or also such formalities which the Code requires under pain of nullity, due provision is made for the various contingencies mentioned by Noone. It is one thing to say that an act is null and is considered as not having been performed; but it is a different matter to label such acts as proceeding from an absolute incompetence of the judge. This kind of incompetence is delineated restrictively in canons 1556-1558. How, then, can there be employed the plaint of nullity against the sentence? This ordinary remedy of the law serves indeed for attacking the nullity of a sentence, but only, so it seems to the writer, in the causes mentioned in canons 1892 and 1894. On other cases the appeal and the plea of *restitutio* is available. The question of whether or not the listings of canons 1892 and 1894 are all-inclusive will be discussed in detail in a later chapter.[56]

Another question touches the matter of judicial prorogation. Prorogation may be defined as the extension of the competence of the jurisdiction of a judge beyond its limits to persons or causes

essential constituents of the act which the sacred canons require under pain of nullity." There are many causes of nullity, but the plaint of nullity against the sentence is not available as a remedy for attacking such nullity. Instead, only the cases mentioned in canons 1892 and 1894 allow for the use of the *querela nullitatis contra sententiam*.

54 *Nullity in Judicial Acts*, pp. 21-25.

55 Cf. *ibid.*, p. 25.

56 Cf. Chapter VII.

not otherwise falling under his competence or jurisdiction.[57] Competence which belongs properly to one judge and is transferred to another judge evinces a prorogation of jurisdiction according to Roberti.[58] Absolute competence cannot be prorogued. An absolutely incompetent tribunal cannot have its jurisdiction extended because it has no jurisdiction to which any extension could be added. If prorogation were valid in this case, there would be question of the conferring of a new jurisdiction, which the law totally disclaims. Therefore, any attempt to prorogue absolute competency causes the resulting sentence to be irremedially null.[59]

Article 2. The Collegiate Tribunal

Canon 1892. *Sententia vitio insanabilis nullitatis laborat, quando.: 1°. Lata est . . . in tribunali collegiali a non legitimo iudicum numero contra praescriptum can. 1576, §1.*

Certain judicial causes must under the sanction of nullity be tried before a collegiate tribunal. The bishop is bound to appoint a diocesan judge (*officialis*) with ordinary power for pronouncing judgment in court, and this *officialis* constitutes one tribunal with the bishop of the diocese. In addition the bishop may give one or more assistants to the diocesan judge. These assistants are called *vice-officiales*.[60] Moreover, in every diocese priests are to be appointed as synodal judges, or pro-synodal judges, if appointed outside of a diocesan synod.[61] A collegiate tribunal ordinarily will consist of the *officialis* or *vice-officialis*, who presides, and two or four of the synodal judges. This tribunal must act as a collegiate body, and pronounce sentence according to the majority vote.[62]

When the obligations contracted through Sacred ordination and also the validity itself of the sacred ordination are impugned, the bill of complaint must be submitted to the Sacred Congrega-

[57] Cf. Burke, *Competence in Ecclesiastical Tribunals*, p. 25.

[58] *De Processibus*, I, n. 60.

[59] Cf. Vermeersch-Creusen, *Epitome*, III, n. 16; canon 1892, 1°.

[60] Cf. canon 1573.

[61] Cf. canons 385-388; 1574.

[62] Cf. canon 1577.

tion of the Sacraments; or, if the validity of the ordination is impugned on account of a substantial defect in the sacred rite, to the Congregation of the Holy Office. The Sacred Congregation (of the Sacraments or of the Holy Office) will decide whether the cause is to be discussed in the form of an ordinary trial or in an informal manner. If the Sacred Congregation decides on a formal trial, it will remand the cause to the tribunal of the diocese which was the proper diocese of the cleric at the time of the ordination in question, except in the case in which the validity of the orders is impugned on account of a substantial defect in the sacred rite, in which event the cause is to be remanded to the tribunal of the diocese in which the ordination took place.[63] If the Sacred Congregation decides on a formal trial, the cause must be submitted to a collegiate tribunal of three judges.[64] The scope of this trial includes everything which may serve to prove or disprove not only the alleged invalidity of the ordination on grounds of want of intention or of a defect in the sacred rite, but also the alleged nullity of the obligations arising from the sacred ordination on grounds of compulsion, extrinsic fear, or any other defect of consent.[65]

Causes involving the bond of marriage must also be tried before a tribunal of three judges.[66] Causes concerning the mere civil

[63] Canon 1993, § 1, 2.

[64] Canon 1576, § 1, 1°. If the Sacred Congregation decides to have the case investigated in an informal manner (*via disciplinari*), it orders the competent tribunal of the diocese to institute the process for the information of the Sacred Congregation, and, after this information has been submitted, the Congregation renders the decision. — Canon 1993, § 3.

[65] Cf. canons 1993; 214; Lega, *Commentarius*, I, (1950) 127; cf. also S.C. de Sacramentis, decr., *Regulae servandae in processibus super nullitate sacrae ordinationis, etc.*, 9 iun. 1931, reg. n. 12. — *AAS*, XXIII (1931), 457-473. Roberti declares that causes which involve the validity of the obligations which normally arise through the reception of sacred orders are not reserved to a collegiate tribunal. He seems to confuse these obligations with the juridical effects consequent on valid matrimony. In view of the plain statement contained in canon 1993, Roberti cannot be followed.

[66] Canon 1576, § 1, 1°. These causes are concerned with the validity of marriage. Excepted from the form of ordinary trials are the causes delineated in canons 1990, 1962 and 1966. Also excepted are the marriages made invalid

consequences of marriage belong to the civil court, if they are brought to court as principal actions; but, if they are incidental or accessory to a cause on the validity or the licitness of a marriage, an ecclesiastical tribunal is competent to try and decide these causes.[67]

Matrimonial causes of the supreme heads of states, of their sons and daughters, and of persons who have the immediate right of succession as heads of states shall be tried by that Sacred Congregation, or Tribunal, or special Committee which the Roman Pontiff will delegate in each individual case.[68] Causes regarding a dispensation from a ratified non-consummated marriage shall be tried by the Sacred Congregation of the Sacraments, and cases of the Pauline privilege by the Sacred Congregation of the Holy Office. Also reserved to the Holy Office is the granting of permission for non-Catholics to act as plaintiffs in matrimonial causes.[69] Wherefore, no lower tribunal can institute proceedings in causes regarding a dispensation from a ratified non-consummated marriage, unless the Holy See has authorized it to proceed. If, however, a competent tribunal has by its own authority conducted a trial to establish the nullity of a marriage on the grounds of the impediment of impotence, and in the course of the trial not impotence but non-consummation of the marriage was proved, the tribunal is to stop judicial proceedings in respect to the cause of nullity and forward all the acts of the case to the Congregation of the Sacraments.[70]

The invalidity of marriages will arise from one of the following reasons: the presence of a diriment impediment;[71] the insuffici-

because of the non-observance of the canonical form of marriage. — Pont. Comm. Interp., Oct. 16, 1919 — *AAS*, XI (1919), 479.

[67] Cf. canons 1961; 1016. The tribunal can decide whether, in view of the nature and gravity of the affair, an incidental cause shall be decided in a formal trial or by a decree. — Canon 1840, §1. Cf. Articles 190-192 of *Matrimonial Instruction of* 1936 — *AAS*, XXVIII (1936), 325 (hereafter referred to as *Instruction*).

[68] Cf. *supra*, Article 1 of this chapter; also canons 1557, § 1, 1°; 1962.

[69] Cf. canons 1962; 247; S.C.S. Off. resp., 27 ian., 1928—*AAS*, XX (1928), 75; 22 mart. 1939 — *AAS*, XXXI (1939), 131.

[70] Cf. canons 1963; *Instruction*, Art. 306.

[71] Cf. canons 1067-1080.

ency of consent,[72] or the lack of canonical form.[73] Questions which involve the effects of the bond of marriage, e.g., the question of separation, or the declaration of free status (*status liber*) are not reserved to a collegiate tribunal if these effects are the principal questions.[74] If the question of the effects of the validity of marriage arises incidentally to a cause which a collegiate tribunal is adjudicating, this tribunal, if it so determines, can decide the incidental question.[75] Canon 1990 specifies the cases in which the local ordinary alone can declare the nullity of marriage. Accordingly, the causes which are mentioned in canon 1990 need not be submitted to a collegiate tribunal.[76] In the causes mentioned in canon 1990, the bishop may declare the nullity of the marriage in summary proceedings, but, if the *defensor vinculi* has good reasons to maintain that there is no certainty about the impediments, or that a dispensation from them has been obtained, he is obliged to appeal to the judge of the court of the second instance, to whom the acts of the cause must then be forwarded, and who is to be reminded by written notice that the cause in question is exempted from the formalities of an ordinary trial.[77] In such causes the judge of the second instance will either confirm the sentence of the first ordinary or order that the cause be tried in the form of an ordinary matrimonial trial, in which event he shall remand the case to the court of the first instance.

[72] Cf. canons 1081-1093.

[73] Cf. canons 1094-1099; *Instruction*, Art. 231.

[74] Cf. Vermeersch-Creusen, *Epitome*, III, 282.

[75] Cf. canon 1840, § 1. Beste declares: "Collegio iudicanti reservantur illae quaestiones tantum, quae rescipiunt ipsum vinculum, non vero illae, quae involvunt vinculi effectus, e.g., de separatione coniugum, de legitimitate natalium, salvo praescripto can. 1962 sq., 1990 et 1993." — *Introductio in Codicem*, p. 785.

[76] Cf. canon 1966. Canon 1990 states: "Cum ex certo et authentico documento, quod nulli contradictioni vel exceptioni obnoxium sit, constiterit de existentia impedimenti disparitatis cultus, ordinis, voti sollemnis castitatis, ligaminis, consanguinitatis, affinitatis aut cognationis spiritualis, simulque pari certitudine apparuerit dispensationem super his impedimentis datam non esse, hisce in casibus, praetermissis sollemnitatibus hucusque recensitis, poterit Ordinarius, citatis partibus, matrimonii nullitatem declarare cum interventu tamen defensoris vinculi."

A collegiate tribunal will then adjudicate the case.[78]

All contentious trials regarding the temporal rights and goods of the cathedral church are to be submitted to a collegiate tribunal of three judges.[79] These temporal rights and goods of the cathedral church are not to be confused with the rights and goods of the chapter, or of the diocesan curia, or of the *mensa episcopalis*, or even of the bishop.[80] They are properly the goods and the rights of the cathedral church itself.[81] Under the name of rights and goods of the cathedral church are understood all those things which are the object of contentious actions — real claims in law which concern the rights that the cathedral church has over lands and goods, and personal judicial actions which are directed against persons themselves to obtain some temporal thing.[82]

The cathedral church is considered in the Code as a non-collegiate moral personality, and is looked upon as consisting of a sacred edifice and various goods and dowries that have been given to it.[83] When the term, *collegiate person*, is employed, the law is concerned with the cathedral chapter,[84] which has its own proper rights and duties as distinct from those of the cathedral church.[85]

The local ordinary may appear in court in the name of the cathedral church.[86] In such causes the bishop is representing the moral personality as such, and the causes are to be adjudicated before a collegiate tribunal.[87] When the question arises concerning the temporal rights and goods of the churches of abbots *nullius*, these causes are likewise to be tried before a collegiate

[77] Cf. canon 1991.

[78] Cf. canon 1992.

[79] Canon 1576, § 1, 1°.

[80] Cf. *supra*, Article 1 of this Chapter; Roberti, *De Processibus*, I, n. 111; Noval, *De Iudiciis*, n. 123.

[81] Cf. canons 1495, § 2; 1497-1499; 1513.

[82] Cf. Lega, *Commentarius*, I, 130; Coronata, *Institutiones Iuris Canonici*, III, n. 1118.

[83] Cf. canons 99; 1161.

[84] Cf. canon 391, § 1.

[85] Cf. canons 391-422; 429-444.

[86] Cf. canon 1653, § 1.

[87] Canon 1576, § 1, 1°.

tribunal. The reason for this is that such churches are equal in the law to cathedral churches. Abbots *nullius* have the same ordinary power and the same obligations as do residential bishops.[88] They have their own chapters[89] or consultors.[90] Their tribunals of the first instance are constituted just as are the tribunals of residential bishops.[91]

In addition, criminal causes which involve an irremovable incumbent's deprivation of a benefice, or the infliction or declaration of excommunication, if prosecuted in a formal trial, must also be adjudicated by a collegiate tribunal of three judges.[92]

An ecclesiastical benefice is a juridical entity, permanently constituted or erected by the competent ecclesiastical authority, and consisting of a sacred office and the right to receive the revenue accruing from the endowment of such office.[93] The incumbent in the benefice can be either removable or irremovable according as the benefice is conferred either revocably or permanently.[94] If a cleric has been appointed as an irremovable incumbent in his benefice,[95] he cannot be judicially deprived[96] of it as a penalty, except in such circumstances in which the law expressly grants this.[97]

In regard to the infliction or declaration or excommunication, such causes must also be tried by a collegiate tribunal if they are

[88] Cf. canon 323. Lega, *Commentarius*, I, (1950) 130.

[89] Cf. canon 324.

[90] Cf. canon 326.

[91] Cf. canons 215, § 2; 1572, § 1; Cf. Lega, *Commentarius*, I, (1950) 130.

[92] Cf. canons 1576, § 1, 1°; 1892, 1°. 1933, § 4, states: "Penances, penal remedies, excommunication, suspension and interdict can be inflicted also by way of precept without judicial procedure, provided the offense is certain." Cf. also canons 2177; 2182 ff.; 2225. Also not subject to a hearing in a formal trial are the offenses spoken of in canons 2168-2194.

[93] Cf. canon 1409.

[94] Cf. canon 1411, 4°.

[95] When a parochial benefice is held by a removable incumbent, the local ordinary can establish him as an irremovable incumbent with the advice of the Cathedral Chapter or the diocesan consultors. — canon 454, § 3.

[96] The irremovable pastor of a benefice can be removed administratively for the reasons mentioned in canon 2147.

[97] Cf. canons 2298, 6°; 2299, § 1. The Code decrees the penal privation of benefice on the part of an irremovable incumbent in certain cases; in canons 2314, § 1, 2° (apostates, heretics and schismatics, who upon being admon-

tried judicially.[98] Excommunication is defined in the Code as a censure by which one is excluded from the communion of the faithful.[99] From the commission of an offense arises an available penal action for the declaration of the penalty decreed in law, i.e., in penalties *latae sententiae*, or for the imposition of the penalty decreed in law, i.e., in penalties *ferendae sententiae*.[100] A condemnatory sentence is that which convicts the defendant, and now inflicts the penalty which was not inflicted before although ordained by law, whereas a declaratory sentence is that which pronounces the crime to have been committed and is retroactive in regard to the penalty, establishing that it was incurred by the very fact of perpetration at the moment that the crime was per-

ished do not repent); 2331, § 2 (conspiracy against the authority of the Pope, his legates or one's own Ordinary); 2340, § 2 (obdurate continuance in censures); 2343, § 2 (the laying of violent hands on a cardinal or on legates of the Pope); 2345 (usurpation of the goods and the rights of the Roman Church); 2346 (usurpation and detention of temporal ecclesiastical goods and property); 2350, § 2 (attempted suicide); 2354, § 2 (offenses against life, liberty and property); 2359, § 3 (sins *contra sextum*; those guilty of concubinage as stated in canon 2359, § 1, follow the manner of procedure in canons 2176-2181); 2368, § 1 (crime of solicitation delineated in can. 904; however, the special procedure prescribed by the Holy Office in the Instruction of June 9, 1922, must be followed. — Cf. Coronata, *Institutiones Iuris Canonici*, IV, n. 2116; Wenrz-Vidal, *Ius Canonicum*, Vol. VII, *Ius Poenale*, n. 510); 2381, 2° (violation of the law of residence; however, extra-judicial procedure is to be followed according to canons 2168-2175); 2406 (unfaithfulness in the custody of records). The privation can be incurred *ipso facto*: cf. canons 2396; 2398; 2266. A tribunal may inflict this penalty: cf. canons 2324; 2336, §1; 2355; 2359, § 3; 2360, § 2; 2394, 2°; 2403; 2405; 2406, § 2.

[98] Cf. canons 1576, § 1, 1°; 1892, 1°. Excommunication can be inflicted also by way of precept without judicial procedure provided the offense is certain — canon 1933, §4. Canon 2225 declares that if a penalty is declared or inflicted by way of judicial sentence, the precepts of the canons relative to the pronouncement of a judicial sentence shall be observed. If, however, a penalty of either *latae* or *ferendae sententiae* has been ordered by way of special precept, it must ordinarily be declared or inflicted in writing or before two witnesses.

In the imposition of penalties attached to a special precept, no judicial proceedings are required.

[99] Cf. canon 2257.

[100] Cf. canon 2210.

petrated.[101]

All criminal causes which necessitate a judicial trial are to be adjudicated in accordance with canons 1552-1959.[102]

Trials in connection with crimes which entail the penalties of deposition, perpetual deprivation of the ecclesiastical garb, or degradation, are reserved to a tribunal of five judges.[103] By deposition a cleric is in addition to other penalties, deprived permanently of all offices, benefices, dignities, pensions and functions in the Church, and becomes unable to acquire them in the future; but he is not deprived of the clerical privileges, nor reduced to the lay state, and he remains bound to the obligations arising from his orders.[104]

The penalty of deposition cannot be inflicted except for the crimes specified in the law.[105]

If the deposed cleric does not show any signs of amendment, the ordinary may deprive him forever of the right to wear the ecclesiastical garb. This entails the loss of the clerical privileges.[106]

Degradation includes deposition, perpetual privation of the ecclesiastical garb and reduction of the cleric to the status of a layman, which implies the loss of the clerical privileges. The degradation may be either verbal or edictal, and is then inflicted by means simply of a sentence, but has immediately all its juridical consequences without any execution, or it may be real or factual, namely when the solemnities and formalities prescribed in the Roman Pontifical are observed.[107]

[101] Cf. canon 2232, §2; Coronata, *Institutiones Iuris Canonici*, III, n. 1394.

[102] Cf. canon 2210.

[103] Canons 1576, § 1, 2°; 1892, 1°.

[104] Cf. canon 2303, § 1; Wernz-Vidal, *Ius Canonicum*, VIII, *Ius Poenale* (Romae, 1937), n. 120 (hereafter cited *Ius Poenale*).

[105] Cf. canon 2303, § 3. This penalty may be or must be inflicted in certain cases: canons 2314, § 1, 2° (obstinate apostasy, heresy, and schism after repeated admonitions); 2320 (desecration of the Sacred Species by clerics); 2322, 1° (simulation of Mass and of the hearing of confessions); 2328 (violation of graves); 2350, § 1 (abortion); 2354, § 2 (certain grave crimes); 2379 (discarding of the clerical garb and tonsure); 2394, 2° (illegal possession of benefice); 2401 (illegal refusal to abandon possession of office, benefice or dignity); 2359, § 2 (certain grave crimes *contra sextum*).

[106] Cf. canon 2304.

[107] Cf. canon 2305, §§ 1, 3.

Degradation can be inflicted only for the crimes designated in the law or on clerics who, having been already deposed and deprived of the clerical habit, continue for a year to give serious scandal.[108] This penalty of degradation is always imposed by means of a condemnatory sentence pronounced by a collegiate tribunal of five judges.[109]

If the tribunal rendering the sentence has not the three or five judges required by canon 1576, §1, the sentence is vitiated with irremediable nullity.[110] When the law of the Code demands that certain cases be adjudicated before a tribunal of three or five judges, one or two judges cannot be sufficient. Canon 1576, §1, states that a collegiate tribunal must try these causes. For the constituting of a collegiate moral personality, there must be at least three physical persons or individuals.[111] In such causes wherein fewer than three or five judges, as prescribed in the law, were to try a cause and to issue a sentence, the sentence itself would be irremediably null,[112] but not all the acts of the cause are null, because the nullity of any one given act does not make null and void the acts which precede or follow, and which do not depend on the invalid act.[113] This statement will have force concerning the entire discussion of a tribunal which adjudicates causes. When a sentence is declared null because of the absolute incompetence of the tribunal, all the acts of the case and of the process are null.[114] When the sentence is declared null because of the lack of the legitimate number of judges, only those acts

[108] Cf. canon 2305, § 2. This penalty is inflicted in the following cases: canons 2314, § 1, 3°. (The formal joining or public adhering of clerics to a non-Catholic sect and their non-amendment after warning); 2343, § 1, 3° (the laying of violent hands on the Pope); 2354, § 2 (voluntary homicide); 2368, § 1 (grave cases of solicitation; however, the special procedure prescribed by the Holy Office in the Instruction of June 9, 1922, must be followed. — Cf. Coronata, *Institutiones Iuris Canonici*, IV, n. 2116; Wernz-Vidal, *Ius Poenale*, n. 510; 2388, § 1 (violation of the obligation of celibacy).

[109] Cf. canon 1576, § 1, 2°; 1892, 1°.

[110] Cf. canon 1892, 1°.

[111] Cf. Canon 100, § 2.

[112] Cf. canon 1892, 1°.

[113] Cf. canon 1680, § 2.

[114] Cf. *supra*, Article 1 of this Chapter; canon 1892, 1°.

are null which in law require the intervention of the whole tribunal, as also the acts which depend thereon.[115]

When such causes as are discussed in this present Article are judicially tried, they are under the sanction of nullity reserved by the law to a collegiate tribunal. Because of this fact the sentence[116] which is issued by fewer than the required number of judges in these causes is irremediably null. As the Code states, every contrary custom is reprobated, and every adverse privilege that had been granted before the Code is revoked.[117]

Though the Code has established the fact that certain causes are reserved to a tribunal of three judges, and certain other causes to a tribunal of five judges,[118] still the law does not definitely impose the obligation that all the steps in the trying of a cause must be handled by the entire collegiate body of judges appointed for the consideration of a particular cause. Indeed, the law seems to indicate that, for the most part, certain of the details, even very important details, like the taking of testimony and the assembling of proofs in a cause, may well be entrusted to an officer of the curia, the *auditor*, and that for all practical purposes only a few important functions, among them the decision to be rendered, are reserved absolutely to the collegiate body of judges.[119]

[115] Cf. Coronata, *Institutiones Iuris Canonici*, III, n. 1418; Wernz-Vidal, *Ius Canonicum*, VI, n. 621, Cf. canons 1577; 1680; 205, § 3.

[116] Canon 1868. The definite sentence settles the principal issue, which was primarily and directly raised by the plaintiff, and not any incidental question arising during the proceedings. The interlocutory sentence is one which the judge pronounces between the beginning of the trial and the definite sentence in order to settle, not the principal cause, but some incidental point which arises and must usually be decided before the trial can proceed (cf. can. 1837). An interlocutory sentence which materially affects the main issue and in such a way as virtually to decide it has definitive force. A decree is any pronouncement of the judge which is not a sentence. The commands, orders, and prohibitions, which are not based on a legal dispute of the litigants and do not judicially close the cause, are classified as decrees. In other words, when the judge issue a decree, he does not need to observe the requirements called for in a judicial trial. — Cf. Lemieux, *The Sentence in Ecclesiastical Procedure*, pp. 5-7.

[117] Cf. canons 1576, § 1; 1577, § 1; 1892, 1°.

[118] Cf. canon 1576, § 1.

[119] Cf. canons 1577, § 1; 1580-1582.

The situation can arise, however, that all the judges of a collegiate tribunal act collegiately in all matters, such as the questioning of the parties and the witnesses, the gathering of proofs, and the like.[120] This procedure is not the usual thing in its occurrence. The Code, however, demands that the collegiate tribunal must act as a body and pronounce sentence according to the majority vote. Before pronouncing any sentence, each of the judges of the tribunal must have in his mind moral certainty about the matter which is to be defined by the sentence. The judge must weigh the proofs according to his conscience.[121]

Lega discusses the eventuality in which a cause is committed for judgment not to three or five but to four or six judges. Certainly it is not essential to the nature of a collegiate tribunal that it should have an unequal number of judges.[122] The writer agrees with Lega in that the sanction of absolute nullity is clearly implied in the text of the law when it is prescribed that there must be a legitimate number of judges. This prescription of law pertains to the public law of the Church, which may not be changed by private authority.[123]

It must be remembered that in all causes in which the sentence is irremediably null because of the lack of the legitimate number of judges, only those acts are null which require the intervention of the whole tribunal.[124]

The elements of the subject matter of canon 1576, §1, and of the requirements of the Code therein established should not be confused with the elements that attend a cause which has been properly decided by a collegiate tribunal, but which carries the signatures of the presiding judge and the notary. Such a sentence would be null and void, but the nullity would be remediable.[125]

[120] Cf. canon 1577, § 1.

[121] Cf. canon 1869.

[122] Cf. Lega, *Commentarius*, II, 1018.

[123] Lega, *loc. cit.*

[124] Cf. canons 1680, § 1; 1892, 1°. Generally those procedural acts which pertain to the drawing up of the acts of the case and which can be committed to an auditor do not require for their validity the presence of the integral tribunal. — Cf. canon 1582; Lega, *Commentarius*, I, 134-135.

[125] Cf. canons 1874, § 5; 1894, 3°.

The local ordinary can commit other causes also to a collegiate tribunal of three or five judges, and he should do so especially when there is question of causes which seem more difficult and are of greater importance in their subject matter by reason of the presence of some specific temporal, local, or personal circumstances or contingencies. The two or four judges who, together with the presiding judge, constitute the collegiate tribunal, are to be chosen by the ordinary from among the synodal judges in rotation, unless he thinks it best to deviate from this rule.[126]

A collegiate tribunal must also judge the causes that concern the temporal rights and goods of the bishop, or of the bishop's benefice (*mensa episcopalis*), or of the diocesan curia. These causes should, with the consent of the bishop, be referred either to the diocesan tribunal of three judges, consisting of the head judge (*officialis*) and two of the older synodal judges, or to the court of second instance.[127]

If the cause in its first instance was tried by a collegiate tribunal, it must also in the court of appeal be tried by a collegiate tribunal, which may not be fewer in number than in the court of the first instance.[128]

The violation of canons 1572, §2, and 1576, §2, in regard to the number of judges constituting a collegiate tribunal does not cause the sentence to be irremediably null, nor is the plaint of nullity against the sentence to be employed in such contingencies. The reason for this statement is that the lack of the legitimate number of judges, which for a remedy looks to the plaint of nullity against the sentence, is concerned only with the prescription of canon 1576, §1.[129]

If a collegiate tribunal adjudicated a cause in line with the provisions of canons 1572, §2, and 1576, §2, then canon 1596 declares that in the appellate instance a collegiate tribunal must also adjudicate their cause. Therefore, the number of judges in the appellate court must not be fewer than the number used in

[126] Canon 1576, §§ 2-3.

[127] Cf. canon 1572, § 2; also *supra*, Article 1 of this Chapter.

[128] Canon 1596.

[129] Cf. canon 1892, 1°; Roberti, *De Processibus*, II, (1 ed.) n. 490.

the court of the first instance.[180] If this rule is violated through the fact that a single judge adjudicated in the appellate instance a cause the hearing of which is governed by the rules expressed in canons 1572, §2, and 1576, §2, the sentence is not vitiated with irremediable nullity, for the rule in canon 1596 does not contain an invalidating clause to that effect.

The situation differs when the rule of canon 1576, §1, is involved. This canon demands either three or five judges for the specific causes mentioned in the canon.[181] Furthermore, if the legitimate number of judges, as prescribed by the law (canon 1576, §1), is not employed the resulting sentence is vitiated with irremediable nullity.[182] If the causes delineated in canon 1576, §1, are carried to the appellate instance, will the sentence of the appellate court be irremedialy null in consequence of the fact that not the legitimate number of judges adjudicated these causes? An example should make the problem clear. Canon 1576, §1, 1°, demands a collegiate tribunal of three judges for marriage causes that are concerned with the validity of the marriage.[183] When the cause comes to the court of the second instance, only one judge is employed. Is the resulting sentence of this one judge irremedialy null? It seems to the writer that the sentence of the appellate court when rendered simply by a single judge is vitiated with irremediable nullity.[184] The reasons for this statement are these: Since canon 1576, §1, 1°, demands three judges under pain of nullity of the sentence in the court of first instance, the same rule must be held as applying in the appellate court.[185] Another reason that confirms this opinion is that the Matrimonial Instruction of 1936[186] makes no distinction between the court of first instance and the appellate court in discussing the requirements of at least three judges for matrimonial causes in which the validity of the bond is at stake.

[180] Cf. canon 1596.
[181] Cf. canon 1576, § 1.
[182] Cf. canon 1892, 1°; cf. also *supra*, p. 59.
[183] Cf. *supra*, p. 52.
[184] Cf. canon 1892, 1°.
[185] Cf. canon 1595.
[186] *Instruction*, art. 13.

One can easily see the purpose of this procedure, since the bond of marriage is too sacred and important a consideration to be entrusted to the decision of one judge.[137]

What has been stated concerning canon 1576, §1, 1°, applies to all the causes mentioned in the first paragraph of canon 1576.[138]

In speaking of causes reserved to a collegiate tribunal, Noone states that if one of the collegiate judges is incapable of receiving or exercising ecclesiastical jurisdiction, or if he was invalidly appointed to the tribunal, or if he has lost his jurisdiction, then the judicial acts of such a tribunal when it has functioned with this disqualified member are just as invalid as if the court had proceeded without the required number of judges.[139] Noone cites canons 1680, §1, and 1892, 1°, as the basis for this statement. The present writer disagrees with Noone in this regard. Canon 1892, 1°, is concerned with the question of absolute incompetence, which is limited to the causes mentioned in canons 1556-1557, and also the lack of the legitimate number of judges as prescribed in canon 1576, §1. In such causes the plaint of nullity can be employed for the purpose of impugning a sentence that is irremediably null. There is in the law no warrant for the use of the plaint of nullity against the sentence in the specific contingency mentioned by Noone.[140]

Article 3. The Right to Stand in Court

Canon 1892. *Sententia vitio insanabilis nullitatis laborat, quando: 2.° Lata est inter partes, quarum altera saltem non habet personam standi in iudicio.*

[137] Cf. Lane, *Matrimonial Procedure in the Ordinary Courts of Second Instance*, p. 73. "Only three judges are necessary for matrimonial causes *de vinculo*. Any additional judges are appointed at the will of the Ordinary, and not in fulfillment of the requirement of the law. Canon 1892, 1°, indicates that a sentence is incurably null only when less than three judges decide a case. . . . If there were only three judges in the court of first instance, it is permitted to have three or five in the second instance." —Lane, *op. cit.*, pp. 74-75.

[138] Cf. *supra*, Article 1 of this Chapter, pp. 58-60.

[139] Cf. Noone, *Nullity in Judicial Acts*, p. 39.

[140] Cf. canons 1680, § 1; 1892, 1°; *infra* Chapter VII.

The sentence would be vitiated with irremediable nullity if rendered in a cause in which at least one of the parties lacked the *ius standi in iudicio*. Therefore, the party's right to a standing in the court is a very important question because of the serious consequences involved.

Judicial capacity, in virtue of which a person can be a party in a trial, is not the same as procedural capacity, in virtue of which a party in a trial can personally perform procedural acts which produce their proper juridical effects. The latter presupposes and completes the former, but is not a necessary consequent of it.[141]

Juridical capacity follows upon a person's baptism, when a man is constituted a person in the Church of Christ with all the rights and duties of Christians, unless, insofar as the rights are concerned, there exists in his life some obstacle that impedes the bond of communion with the Church, or a censure which the Church has inflicted upon him.[142]

Inasmuch as the Code presupposes juridical capacity, and thereupon legislates concerning the procedural capacity of a party to act in court,[143] it will not be necessary to go into a detailed discussion except in regard to procedural capacity. By procedural capacity is meant that right in virtue of which a party in a trial can personally perform procedural acts which produce their proper juridical effects.[144] According to Roberti, procedural capacity is sometimes referred to as *legitimatio ad processum*.[145] It is an intrinsic quality that is demanded in a party who intends to act personally in a trial.[146]

[141] Cf. Krol, *The Defendant in Contentious Trials*, The Catholic University of America Canon Law Studies, n. 146 (The Catholic University of America Press, Washington, D.C.: 1942), p. 66.

[142] Cf. canon 87.

[143] Roberti, *De Processibus*, I, (2. ed.) n. 197; Noone, *Nullity in Judicial Acts*, p. 51.

[144] Cf. Krol, *The Defendant in Contentious Trials*, p. 66; Wernz-Vidal, *Ius Canonicum*, VI, n. 203.

[145] *De Processibus*, I, (2. ed.) n. 197.

[146] Hanssen, "De Sanctione Nullitatis in processu Canonico," — *Appollinaris* (Romae, 1928-), XI (1938), 255.

SECTION 1. MINORS

Every person not prohibited by the sacred canons may bring a suit as plaintiff.[147] Procedural capacity, however, is denied to minors in a trial.[148] If minors are parties to a trial either as plaintiffs or as defendants, the sentence that concludes such a trial would be irremediably null.[149] The Code establishes that parents and guardians are bound to plead or defend the causes of minors.[150] The writer agrees with Krol when he states that these minors are not merely to be assisted or authorized to act in a trial by their parents or guardians, but they are to be represented in the trial by their parents and guardians.[151] The reason for this restriction on minors is that only a person of major age is entitled to the full exercise of his rights, and, as a result, minors must remain subject to their parents or guardians in the exercise of their rights, except in matters in which the law holds them exempt from paternal power.[152]

If the judge thinks that the rights of minors are in conflict with the rights of the parents or guardians, or that they live at so great a distance from the parents or guardians that the latter cannot at all, or can only with great difficulty, represent their charges in court, a guardian *ad litem* is to be appointed by the judge.[153] In spiritual causes, however, or in causes connected with spiritual affairs,[154] minors who are over fourteen years of

[147] Canon 1646.

[148] Cf. canon 1648, § 1. The Code (canon 88) decrees that a person who has completed his twenty-first year is called a major; under twenty-one, he is called a minor. A boy is regarded as having reached the age of puberty when he completes his fourteenth year; a girl, when she completes her twelfth.

[149] Cf. canon 1892, 2°.

[150] Cf. canon 1648, § 1.

[151] Cf. *Defendants in Contentious Trials*, p. 69.

[152] Cf. canon 89.

[153] Cf. canon 1648, § 2; Lega, *Commentarius*, I, (1950), 305.

[154] In regard either to spiritual causes or to causes connected with spiritual affairs, Lega stated the following: "Hae sunt causae beneficiales, matrimoniales, s. ordinationis, aut professionis religiosae, causae respicientes status electionem sive sacerdotalis sive religiosi, aut iura patronatus." — *Commentarius*, I, (1950), 306.

age have full, independent, procedural capacity, if they have attained the use of reason. In the same causes minors who are under fourteen years of age and have attained the use of reason can sue and defend without the consent of the parents or guardians, but they must act through a procurator *ad litem* chosen by the minor with the approval of the ordinary, or through a guardian *ad litem* appointed by the ordinary.[155]

If a guardian has already been appointed for a minor by the civil authority, such a guardian can be admitted into court by the ecclesiastical law, provided the consent of the proper ordinary of that person is had. If the ordinary deems it prudent, he can appoint a special guardian *ad litem* for the ecclesiastical trial.[156] If the guardian *ad litem* is not effective in defending the rights of the minor or does not perform his duties properly, the judge is obliged to assign an advocate to protect the rights of the minor.[157] When minors reach their majority, which comes at twenty-one years, they come into the full exercise of their rights.[158]

SECTION 2.

THE INSANE, PRODIGALS, AND WEAK-MINDED PERSONS

Persons who lack the use of reason do not enjoy procedural capacity.[159] Persons habitually devoid of the use of reason are regarded by the law as equivalent to infants. Therefore, infants[160] and the insane lack procedural capacity. Parents and guardians

[155] Cf. canon 1648, § 3; Roberti, *De Processibus*, I, (2. ed.) n. 201. A guardian is given to a person who is incapable of acting legally because of a deficiency in his age. — Coronata, *Institutiones Iuris Canonici*, III, n. 1174. A procurator is a personal representative of the plaintiff or the defendant, and is properly styled *procurator ad litem*. — Woywod, *A Practical Commentary on the Code of Canon Law* (Revised and enlarged edition by Callistus Smith, 2 vols., New York: Joseph F. Wagner, Inc. 1948), II, n. 1629.

[156] Cf. canon 1651; Roberti, *De Processibus*, I, (2. ed.) n. 201.

[157] Cf. canon 1655, §2; Lega, *Commentarius*, I, (1950), 307.

[158] Canon 89.

[159] Cf. canon 1648, § 1.

[160] Canon 88, § 3: Impubes, ante plenum septennium dicitur infans . . . et censetur non sui compos.

are bound to plead or defend the causes of infants, and curators are to plead or defend the causes of persons who are insane.[161]

If a judge thinks that the rights of such persons are in conflict with the rights of the parents, guardians, or curators, or that they live at so great a distance from the parents, guardians, or curators that the latter cannot at all, or can only with great difficulty, represent their charges in court, a guardian *ad litem* is to be appointed by the judge in the cause of infants, and a curator *ad litem* in the cause of the insane. Previously appointed guardians and others so constituted lack the right to represent their wards after the appointment of a guardian *ad litem* or a curator *ad litem*.[162]

Persons who because of their spendthrift habits (prodigals) as also weak-minded persons have but a limited procedural capacity, since the Code permits them to appear personally in court only to answer for their offenses, or at the order of the judge.[163] Apart from these exceptional cases, prodigals and weak-minded persons must sue and be sued through their curator. Otherwise the sentence would be irremediably null, because they would lack the right of any standing in court.[164] Curators assigned to prodigals and weak-minded persons by the civil authority can be admitted by the ecclesiastical judge into court, but only with the consent of the ward's proper ordinary. If after mature reflection, the proper ordinary thinks it prudent, he may appoint another curator for the ecclesiastical forum.[165] When the civil authority has determined in a particular cause either that a party is a prodigal or that he is weak-minded, the ecclesiastical judge can follow that judgment, but he has no obligation to do so from law.[166] If the

[161] Cf. canon 1648, § 1. A curator is appointed to take care of persons who because of mental deficiency or for other reasons are unable to attend to their own interests.—Coronata, *Institutiones Iuris Canonici*, III, n. 1174; Wernz-Vidal, *Ius Canonicum*, VI, n. 207.

[162] Cf. canon 1648, § 2; Roberti, *De Processibus*, I, (2. ed.) n. 201.

[163] Cf. canon 1650.

[164] Cf. canons 1650; 1892, 2°.

[165] Cf. canons 1651; 105.

[166] Coronata, *Institutiones Iuris Canonici*, III, n. 1176; Roberti, *De Processibus*, I, (2. ed.) n. 202.

judge does not follow the judgment of the civil authority, what procedure must the judge follow in order to determine who are to be considered as prodigals or weak-minded persons? The Code of Canon Law does not determine this question.[167] The Pontifical Commission for the Authentic Interpretation of the Code has declared that in order to assign a curator to those who are destitute of the use of reason or who are weak-minded, a regular trial is not required, but rather a decree, given by the ordinary after he has prudently investigated the matter, is sufficient.[168] The prudent investigation on the part of the ordinary may consist in an interview with the ward, his family and relatives, in an examination of the ward by experts, and in an inspection of all available documents on the subject.[169] It seems that upon such investigation the ordinary can declare someone a prodigal or a weak-minded persons, and then by means of a decree appoint a curator. It is from the moment of this decree that prodigals and weak-minded persons lose their procedural capacity. If, however, the one who is declared a spendthrift or a weak-minded person contests the action of the ordinary, then such a person has a right for a formal judicial process.[170]

If, contrary to the decree of the ordinary, prodigals or weak-minded persons sue or are sued in court, and these are not represented by curators, the sentence of such a trial would be irremediably null,[171] unless the prodigals or weak-minded persons appeared in court to answer for their own offenses, or by order of the judge.[172]

When a conflict between the rights of the prodigal or weak-minded person and the rights of the appointed curator develops, the judge can appoint a curator *ad litem*. The same procedure can be followed if the curator lives at a great distance and can

[167] Cf. Coronata, *loc. cit.*

[168] Cf. resp., 25 ian. 1943 — *AAS*, XXXV (1943), 58.

[169] Cf. Noone, *Nullity in Judicial Acts*, p. 54.

[170] Cf. Roberti, *De Processibus*, I, (2. ed.) n. 202; Coronata, *Institutiones Iuris Canonici*, III, n. 1176.

[171] Cf. canon 1892, 2°.

[172] Cf. canon 1650.

only with great difficulty represent his charge in court.[173]

Section 3. Religious

Without the consent of their superiors, the members of religious communities have no personal standing in court.[174] The phrase, members of religious communities, embraces all members of religious communities both those of solemn vows and those of simple vows, since the law does not distinguish between them.[175] Canon 488, 7°, declares that members of religious communities are those persons who have taken vows in any religious community. All others, therefore, are not affected by this lack of procedural capacity.[176]

The members of religious communities do not need the consent of their superiors if they bring suit against the religious organization in order to vindicate the rights which they acquired by profession, e.g., the participation in the spiritual benefits and favors of the community.[177] Nor is the superior's consent necessary when the members of religious communities desire to denounce their superior judicially, e.g., because of some delict or malfeasance that the superior has committed. In such causes the member of the religious community denounces his superior to the promoter of justice, and must give aid to the promoter of justice to prove the crime.[178]

Finally, the consent of the superior is not required if a member of the religious community legitimately lives outside the religious house, and the defense of his rights becomes urgent.[179] Thus, if any member of the religious community suffers some injury or

[173] Cf. canon 1648, § 2.

[174] Cf. canon 1652.

[175] Cf. Lega, *Commentarius*, I, (1950) 313.

[176] Cf. canons 488, 7°; 1652. Novices and those who lead a community life without vows do not lose their procedural capacity. — canon 673, § 1.

[177] Cf. canon 1652, 1°; Roberti, *De Processibus*, I, (2. ed.) n. 207.

[178] Cf. canon 1652, 3°. "Actio seu accusatio criminalis uni promotori iustitiae, ceteris omnibus exclusis, reservatur." — canon 1934. "Qui delictum denuntiat debet promotori iustitiae adiumenta suppeditare ad eiusdem delicti probationem." — canon 1937.

[179] Cf. canon 1652, 2°.

has some object stolen from him, he can immediately bring an action in court without the consent of the superior.[180] The reason for this procedure is that the consent is presumed and is also considered as given when permission has been granted for outside the religious house.[181] When a member of a religious community is raised to the episcopal dignity, or is given the care of souls in a parish, he does not lack the right to stand in court in order to protect the rights and goods of the parish, or those rights which he acquired through the episcopate.[182]

If a member of a religious community enters into a contract, but does not have the necessary permission of his superiors, he is personally liable, and not the religious organization.[183] Though he is personally liable in such cases, he still cannot stand in court unless he has the consent of his superior. The reason is that the Code states that a member of a religious community without the consent of his superior does not have the right to stand in court.[184] If nevertheless a member of a religious community is sued and goes to court without the required permission of his superior, the sentence that concludes such a trial is vitiated with irremediable nullity.[185] Even though Wernz-Vidal state that a person who is professed with simple vows in a religious community can be sued without the consent of his superior for a debt which such a person unlawfully contracted,[186] the law itself makes no such distinction between members professed with solemn or with simple vows when it declares that without the consent of the superior the member of the religious community lacks procedural capacity whether he be plaintiff or defendant.[187]

[180] Cf. Lega, *Commentarius*, I, (1950) 318.

[181] Cf. Lega, *loc. cit.*; Roberti, *De Processibus*, I, (2. ed.) n. 207.

[182] Cf. Lega, *loc. cit.*; Roberti, *loc. cit.*

[183] Cf. canon 536, §§ 2, 3.

[184] Cf. canon 1652. Canon 1646 declares: "Reus autem legitime conventus respondere debet." The writer believes that in such cases the plaintiff's right to sue the member of a religious community overrides every right a superior may have in withholding consent for the prospective defendant's appearance in court. Cf. Roberti, *De Processibus*,, I, n. 207.

[185] Cf. canon 1892, 2°.

[186] Cf. Wernz-Vidal, *Ius Canonicum*, VI, n. 207.

[187] Cf. canon 1652; Lega, *Commentarius*, I, (1950) 316, n. 7.

Though the Code of Canon Law declares that a member of a religious community who is dwelling lawfully outside his religious house can appear in court without the consent of his superior when the defense of his rights becomes urgent,[188] does this imply that when he is unlawfully absent from his house as a fugitive or as an apostate he needs the consent of the superior to appear in court?[189] It seems that the superior's consent is required in the contentious cause of a fugitive or apostate member of a religious community.[190] Members of an Order who have committed a crime outside their house, and are not punished by their superior after he has been informed of the fact, may be punished by the local ordinary.[191] Since the superior can and actually does punish a fugitive or apostate member of the community with suitable punishments, the relationship between the superior and the fugitive or apostate certainly is not severed because of the unlawful departure of the latter.[192] In such cases of punishment therefore, the consent of the superior is necessary for the fugitive or the apostate to have a standing in court.[193]

If in a trial a fugitive or an apostate member of a religious community does not have the necessary consent of the superior for a standing in court, there seems to be a miscarriage of justice if such persons are able to employ the plaint of nullity against an unfavorable sentence. In other words, they could profit from their wrong-doing. The writer agrees with Krol in stating that sound principles of law demand that the malice of a person should not redound to his favor or to the detriment of others, nor should

[188] Cf. canon 1652, 2°.

[189] Canon 644, § 1: "Apostata a religione dicitur professus a votis perpetuis sive sollemnibus sive simplicibus qui e domo religiosa illegitime egreditur cum animo non redeundi, vel qui, etsi legitime egressus, non redit eo animo ut religiosae obedientiae sese subtrahat.

§ 2. Malitiosus animas, de quo in § 1, iure praesumitur, si religiosus intra mensem nec reversus fuerit nec Superiori animum redeundi manifestaverit.

§ 3. Fugitivus est qui, sine Superiorum licentia, domum religiosam deserit cum animo ad religionem redeundi."

[190] Cf. canon 1652, 2°.

[191] Cf. canon 616, § 2.

[192] Cf. canons 2385; 2386.

[193] Cf. canon 1892, 2°.

it interfere with the proper administration of justice.[194]

Inasmuch as the members of religious Orders who are unlawfully absent from their house do not enjoy the privilege of exemption,[195] they appear to be subject to the local ordinary in virtue of canon 500, §1. Therefore, if the consent of the superior cannot be had, then the consent of the local ordinary should be secured in order to give such persons a rightful standing in court.[196]

All members of religious communities are held to respond personally for their own crimes, since the crimes of a person ought never to redound to the detriment of the Church. Therefore, they can be sued for damages arising from their crimes, whether or not the consent of the superior is had.[197]

Section 4. Moral Personalities

Moral personalities, either collegiate or non-collegiate, are considered minors by the law,[198] and therefore lack the personal right of standing in court. These moral or legal personalities are to be represented in court by their rector or administrator.[199] If the rights of the legal personality conflict with those of the rector or the administrator, the ordinary shall designate a procurator to represent the moral personality.[200]

[194] Cf. Krol, *The Defendant in Contentious Trials*, p. 73.

[195] Cf. canon 616, § 1.

[196] Cf. Krol, *loc. cit.* The non-exempt religious are subject to the ordinary by law. — Cf. canon 500, § 1.

[197] Roberti, *De Processibus*, I, (2. ed.) n. 207. Lega presented this commentary: "Quamvis hic canon (1652) non expresse dicat at subintelligitur, quippe est omnino extra controversiam atque certis ex principiis fluens, nempe ipsum religiosum respondere debere nedum de delictis sed etiam civilibus, quos vocant, derivantibus ex delicto: can. 2210, n. 2. Asseruimus autem haec non esse aliena a canonis 1652 praescripto." — *Commentarius*, I, (1950) 316.

[198] Cf. canon 100, § 3; Coronata, *Institutiones Iuris Canonici*, III, n. 1175.

[199] Cf. canon 1649.

[200] Canon 1649. Lega pointed to an example of a conflict of interest in a cause between the moral personality and a blood relative of its rector. Since the rector may be in sympathy with his relative and, as a result, suspected of not defending properly the rights of the moral personalities which he represents, the ordinary must appoint a procurator to represent the moral personality. — *Commentarius*, I, 307.

If moral personalities are not legally represented in a trial, then the sentence of the trial is vitiated with irremediable nullity.[201] Therefore, it is necessary to consider the representation of moral personalities in judicial trials.

First to be considered are non-collegiate moral personalities.[202] The local ordinary may appear in court in the name of the cathedral church or of the *mensa episcopalis;* but, to act licitly, the local ordinary must consult the cathedral chapter (diocesan consultors) or the board of administration, securing their advice or their consent according to the amount of money involved in the case, as prescribed by canon 1532, §§2, 3.[203] In these cases the requisite consent or consultation that is mentioned does not pertain to the validity of the process, for canon 1635, §1, expressly declares that the seeking of their advice or the gaining of their consent stands as a condition for the lawfulness of the ordinary's plea or defense in court.

All beneficiaries have a standing in court in the name of their benefice, but to act licitly they must observe the rule of canon 1526, which demands the written permission of the local ordinary.[204]

A collegiate church litigates in court through a representative of the collegiate chapter, and other churches, if they are of autonomous status, through their rectors.[205] Parishes, which as bene-

[201] Cf. canon 1892, 2°; Lega, *Commentarius*, I, (1950) 308.

[202] Cf. canon 99.

[203] Cf. canon 1653, § 1. The formalities demanded in canon 1532, §§2, 3, for the alienation of ecclesiastical goods do not *per se* pertain to the representation in court. — Lega, *Commentarius*, I, (1950) 321.

[204] Canon 1653, § 2. In urgent cases there should be obtained at least the consent of the rural deans, who shall at once inform the local ordinary of the permission granted. — Canon 1526.

[205] Cf. Roberti, *De Processibus*, I, (2. ed.) n. 205. Roberti states that the written permission of the ordinary according to canon 1526 is required in certain cases, e.g., when churches of autonomous status (*sui iuris*) are involved in court procedure. To act otherwise makes the acts to be null. He cites canon 1527, which declares that administrators act invalidly in suits which deal with matters that exceed the limits of the ordinary administration, unless they first obtain the faculty in writing from the local ordinary. This provision, however, does not extend to acts of litigation, for canon 1653, § 2, expressly declares that the permission of the ordinary is needed only for lawfulness, not for validity. — *Loc. cit.*

fices are united to a moral personality are to be represented not by those who actually have the care of souls, but rather by those who represent the moral personality itself, e.g., by him who represents the collegiate chapter or the religious community.[206] The diocesan seminary is to be represented in court by its rector, or by the *oeconomus* in those things that pertain to its temporal goods. The representation of hospitals, orphanages, and similar institutions dedicated to works of religion or charity is governed according to the norms of their charter.[207]

If the non-collegiate moral personality is not legally represented in court, the sentence which concludes such a trial is vitiated with irremediable nullity.[208]

Next to be considered are collegiate moral personalities.[209] Prelates and the superiors of chapters, of sodalities and of any other college have no standing in court in the name of their community, unless they have obtained its consent in the manner defined by its statutes.[210] By the term "prelates" the law points to clerics, secular or religious, who have ordinary jurisdiction in the external forum.[211] The superiors of the chapters herein referred to are the immediate superiors as determined by the constitution of the chapters. The chapters here referred to are secular ones, moral personalities other than religious communities. The superiors of sodalities and of other colleges are either the rectors or the administrators of these moral personalities as determined by the constitutions of these collegiate bodies.[212] The statutes here referred to are based on the franchise or the certificate of incorporation, or on the decree of establishment issued by the competent ordinary.[213]

There are some authors[214] who interpret the clause of canon

[206] Cf. Roberti, *loc. cit.*; Wernz-Vidal, *Ius Canonicum*, VI, n. 209.

[207] Cf. canons 1489, § 3; 1649.

[208] Cf. canon 1892, 2°.

[209] Cf. canon 100, §§ 2, 3.

[210] Cf. canons 1653, § 3; 105.

[211] Cf. canon 110.

[212] Cf. canons 110; 410. Also cf. Noval, *De Iudiciis*, n. 258.

[213] Kilkullen, *The Collegiate Moral Person as Party Litigant*, p. 102.

[214] Noval, *De Iudiciis*, n. 258; Lega, *Commentarius*, I, (1950) 323.

1653, §3, i.e., "*sine eiusdem consensu ad normam statutorum,*" as providing that the consent is always required unless the statutes state otherwise; but there are other authors[215] who maintain that the consent is not required unless the statutes expressly demand it. The latter authors believe their opinion is better because in the preliminary drafts of the Code there was a clause which provided that the consent of the community was required unless the statutes stated otherwise, but this clause does not appear in the Code.[216] The writer disagrees with both of these opinions. If the words of canon 1653, §3, are taken both in text and in context,[217] they mean but one thing according to the writer, namely that the consent is always required, but that the manner of securing this consent is defined in the statutes by which the moral personality is governed.

Since this consent of the community is required for validity, the prelate or superior who acts in a trial without it gives cause to nullity in the resulting sentence.[218] The consent of the community in such cases does not excuse the superiors from the necessity of securing the written permission of the ordinary before

[215] Roberti, *De Processibus*, I, (2. ed.) n. 240; Krol, *The Defendant in Contentious Trials*, p. 75; Kilcullen, *The Collegiate Moral Person as Party Litigant*, p. 103.

[216] Cf. Roberti, *Schemata*, G. can. 113, § 3; F. can. 115, § 1; D. can. 130, § 1; C. can. 105, § 1, as given on pp. 140-141.

[217] Cf. canon 18.

[218] Cf. canons 1653, §3; 1892, 2°; 105. There are some who think that if the statutes require the consent of the community for lawfulness, the sentence of a trial would not be invalid. — Noval, *De Iudiciis*, n. 258. This opinion cannot be admitted, since it is contrary to the Code. The nullity of a trial is a matter of public law and should, therefore, be determined by the Code rather than by the statutes of a particular community. — cf. Krol, *The Defendant in Contentious Trials*, p. 76. The Code leaves the community free to determine by its statutes whether or not the consent is required, but once the statutes prescribe its necessity, canon 1653, § 3, makes it necessary for the validity of the representation. — Roberti, *De Processibus*, I, n. 204; Coronata, *Institutiones Iuris Canonici*, III, n. 1175; Noone, *Nullity in Judicial Acts*, p. 63. This opinion is not in conformity with the words of the Code because the consent of the community is always required, so that the statutes merely determine the manner of securing that consent, but not whether or not the consent itself is required.

entering upon the trial.[219]

If the prelates or superiors take their stand in the court without the consent or permission prescribed by canon 1653, then these communities and colleges have the right to hold the superiors or representatives liable for any damages.[220]

The local ordinary himself may either in person or by proxy act in court for the legal personalities subject to his jurisdiction, whenever their administrators fail to defend them, or prove negligent in the defense of their rights.[221] Since the law declares that the local ordinary has the duty of diligently supervising the administration of all ecclesiastical goods in his territory,[222] does the ordinary, in his supervisory character, have a standing in Court for the moral personalities in virtue of canon 1519, §1, when there is question of failure to act, or of negligence on the part of the administrator, or does canon 1653, §5, confer a new designation on the ordinary as an extraordinary administrator? The writer agrees with the opinion of Lega that the local ordinary acts in such cases as an extraordinary administrator in the name of the legal personality. The reason for this opinion is based on the words of the Code, "*in iudicio nomine personae moralis,*" as indicating an extraordinary administrator.[223]

Superiors of religious organizations cannot act in court for their communities, except in the manner prescribed by the constitutions of their organization.[224] These superiors include those

[219] Cf. canon 1526.

[220] Cf. canon 1653, § 4. Cf. also canon 2210, § 2, on tort actions for the reparation of losses as well as criminal actions.

[221] Cf. canon 1653, § 5. There are various reasons that can cause this failure or negligence on the part of the administrator, e.g., the death or sickness of the administrator, his lack of capacity or skill in such matters, or his failure to fulfill the obligations prescribed in canon 1523. — Lega, *Commentarius*, I, 325.

[222] Cf. canon 1519, § 1.

[223] Cf. Lega, *Commentarius*, I, (1950) 326. Roberti believes that the local ordinary would act in his public capacity for the protection of the ecclesiastical goods of the moral personalities under his jurisdiction. — *De Processibus*, I, (2. ed.) n. 206. Lega declared furthermore that the local ordinary should by decree state his intention of acting for the moral personality in accordance with canon 1653, § 5. — *Loc. cit.*

[224] 224 Cf. canon 1653, § 6.

persons who have particular power to watch over the rights of the organization and to administer the temporalities of the organization. These superiors in religious institutes, whether of men religious or of women religious, include not only the superiors general, but also the superiors of the particular provinces and houses of the institute.[225]

If in the name of collegiate or non-collegiate moral personalities anyone other than their lawful representative or administrator sought a standing in court, then the sentence which concludes such a trial would be vitiated with irremediable nullity.[226]

Section 5. Excommunicated Persons

Excommunicated persons who are to be shunned (*excommunicati vitandi*) and all excommunicated persons subsequent to a declaratory or condemnatory sentence of excommunication against them may personally enter a suit in court only with a view to attacking the justice or the legality of their excommunication; through a procurator they may act in court to avert any other spiritual harm; in all other causes it is not allowable for them to enter a suit in ecclesiastical courts. Other excommunicated persons are generally acknowledged a standing in court.[227]

It should be noted that no excommunicated person is branded as a *vitandus*, unless (1) the excommunication has been pronounced on him by name by the Apostolic See; (2) the excommunication has been publicly announced and (3) the fact that he must be shunned is mentioned in the decree or the sentence. All three conditions must be present.[228]

A condemnatory sentence is that which upon conviction of the defendant and only thereupon, inflicts the penalty for which the law has made specific provision, whereas a declaratory sentence

[225] Cf. Lega, *Commentarius*, I, (1950) 326; Noval, *De Iudiciis*, n. 261.

[226] Cf. canon 1892, 2°.

[227] Canon 1654.

[228] Cf. canon 2258, § 1. The only exception in the Code points to the case in which a person would become a *vitandus*, quite apart from the realization of the conditions, by laying violent hands on the person of the Roman Pontiff. The penalty is incurred *ipso facto*. — Canon 2343, § 1, 1°.

is that which upon official verification of the perpetrated delict confirms the existence of the already incurred penalty, the inception of which reaches back to the moment when the delict was committed.[229]

In regard to any rightful standing in court, all excommunicated persons who are to be shunned (*vitandi*) and all excommunicated persons against whom a declaratory or a condemnatory sentence of excommunication has been pronounced, are permitted only to impugn the justice or the legality of their excommunication.[230] Through the agency of a procutator they may institute court proceedings to avert any other spiritual harm, e.g., to impugn the validity of their marriage.[231] In all other matters they are to be rejected.[232] Roberti is of the opinion that these excommunicated persons (the *vitandi* and also the *tolerati* after a declaratory or a condemnatory sentence) do not have any rightful standing in court in trials that are concerned with other matters than the impugning of the justice of their excommunication or the averting of spiritual harm. The consequence of this opinion would be that the resulting sentence would be vitiated with irremediable nullity.[233]

It is to be noted that by baptism a person becomes a subject of the Church of Christ with all the rights and duties of a Christian, unless, insofar as the rights are concerned, there exists in his life some obstacle that impedes the bond of communion with the

[229] Cf. canon 2232, § 2; Coronata, *Institutiones Iuris Canonici*, III, n. 1394. "Si poena declaretur vel infligatur per sententiam iudicialem, serventur canonum praescripta circa sententiae iudicialis pronuntiationem; si vero poena latae vel ferendae sententiae inflicta sit ad modum praecepti particularis, scripto aut coram duobus testibus ordinarie declaretur vel irrogetur, indicatis poenae causis, salvo praescripto can. 2193." — Canon 2225.

[230] Cf. canon 1654, § 1.

[231] Cf. canon 1654, § 1; Lega, *Commentarius*, I, n. 330; Roberti, *De Processibus*, I, n. 208.

[232] Cf. canon 1654, § 1.

[233] Cf. Roberti, *De Processibus*, I, n. 208; also cf. Wernz-Vidal, *Ius Canonicum*, VI, n. 206. Noone believes that this opinion is too rigorous, and that these persons do have the absolute right of a standing in court. He argues from the pre-Code law, and cites Lega as in agreement with his opinion.—*Nullity in Judicial Acts*, pp. 66-67.

Church, or a censure which the Church has inflicted upon him.[234] It seems to the writer that Roberti's opinion is the correct one, for the censure of excommunication is actually a most serious obstacle which would bar such persons for the right of acting in court; and, in the words of the Code, it is not allowable for them to enter a suit in ecclesiastical courts.[235] Furthermore, the wording of canon 1654, §2, seems indirectly to indicate as much when it states: "*Alii excommunicati generatim stare in iudicio queunt.*" If other excommunicated persons generally are acknowledged a standing in court, it seems that those who are *vitandi* and also the *tolerati* after a declaratory or condemnatory sentence cannot have any standing in court, with the exception of the two indicated instances — an impugning of the justice of their excommunication and the averting of spiritual harm.[236]

The second group of excommunicated persons consists of all those who, though they are excommunicated, cannot be designated as *vitandi* or at least as *tolerati* after a declaratory or a condemnatory sentence.[237] This group is generally acknowledged a standing in court.[238] The exception of excommunication can, however, be raised by the opposing party at any stage of the trial, and consequently these persons may be excluded from the suit.[239] Canon 1654, §2, is modified by canon 1628, which gives the opposing party the right to raise the exception of excommunication. The sense of canon 1654, §2, is, therefore, that other excommunicated persons may act in court unless the exception of excommunication is raised against them.[240]

In regard to excommunicated persons who are summoned as defendants, canon 1654 is silent; but canon 1646 declares that

[234] Cf. canon 87.

[235] Cf. canons 1654, § 1; 2263.

[236] Cf. canon 1654.

[237] "Cui sententiae aequiparatur irrogatio poenae per praeceptum particulare ad tenorem can. 2225." — Beste, *Introductio in Codicem*, p. 801. Cf. *supra*, Section 5 of this Chapter, p. 78.

[238] Canon 1654, § 2. "Alii excommunicati generatim stare in iudicio queunt." Cf. canon 2263: ". . . nequit in causis ecclesiasticis agere, nisi ad normam can. 1654."

[239] Cf. canon 1628, § 3; Noval, *De Iudiciis*, n. 263.

the defendant who is legitimately sued must answer. Therefore, all excommunicated persons must appear in court when they are summoned as defendants, since no one should derive profit from his excommunication by not appearing in court.

In order that the plaintiff and the defendant will have a rightful standing in court (*ius standi in iudicio*), the provisions of canons 1646-1654, as they are discussed above in detail, must be observed. If it is proved that either party to a suit does not have any rightful standing in court, then the resulting sentence of such a trial will be vitiated with irremediable nullity.[241]

Section 6. Status of Non-Catholics

By baptism a man is constituted a person in the Church of Christ with all the rights and duties of Christians, unless, insofar as the rights are concerned, there exists in his life some obstacle that impedes the bond of communion with the Church, or a censure which the Church has inflicted upon him.[242] It must be noted that the Code simply declares that all baptized persons are subject to the laws of the Church. No distinction is made between persons who are baptized in the Catholic Church and those who are validly baptized in non-Catholic sects.[243] Baptized non-Catholics are in principle subject to the Church. Even doubtfully baptized persons are presumed to be subjects of the Church if the fact of baptism is certain but the validity of its administration is in doubt. The reason for this presumption is that validity must be presumed unless there are reasons which contradict this

[240] If the plaintiff is a *vitandus* or a *toleratus* after a declaratory or a condemnatory sentence, it is not necessary for the defendant to raise the exception — though he may — because the judge must always exclude him *ex officio*. — Canon 1628, § 3.

[241] Cf. canon 1892, 2°.

[242] Cf. Canon 87.

[243] Cf. Cappello, "De Acatholicorum Incapacitate Agendi in Foro Ecclesiastico," *Miscellanea Vermeersch* (2 vols., Romae: Pontificia Universita Gregoriana, 1935), I, 394 (hereafter referred to as "De Acatholicorum Incapacitate."

presumption.[244] Canon 87, however, states that as far as the rights are concerned, there may be some obstacle that impedes the bond of communion with the Church.[245]

In regard to infidels, such persons possess neither juridical nor processual capacity. Because of this lack of capacity, infidels generally do not have any rightful standing in court.[246] Since these infidels are not directly subject to the jurisdiction of the Church, they cannot be sued for any cause before the tribunals of the Church.[247] Infidels, however, may at times become indirectly subject to the Church, e.g., through their relationship with persons or through some attendant connection with a cause which belongs to the Church as a spiritual matter. This occurs most frequently in matrimonial causes.[248]

It must be noted that to the Holy Office is reserved the right to permit non-Catholics, whether baptized or unbaptized, to act as plaintiffs in matrimonial causes.[249]

Authors are generally agreed that, if an infidel acted as plaintiff in an ecclesiastical court without any permission, he would lack

[244] Cf. Coronata, *Institutiones Iuris Canonici*, I, n. 14; Woywod, *A Practical Commentary on the Code of Canon Law*, I, n. 65.

[245] Cf. Coronata, *Institutiones Iuris Canonici*, III, n. 1173; Wernz-Vidal, *Ius Canonicum*, VI, 210.

[246] Cf. canon 87; Doheny, *Canonical Procedure*, I, 128.

[247] Cf. Ottaviani, *Institutiones Iuris Publici Ecclesiastici*, I, n. 160.

[248] Cf. Bourque, *The Judicial Power of the Church*, p. 124.

[249] Cf. *Instruction*, art. 35. Cf. also S.C.S. Off. resp., 27 ian. 1928 — *AAS*, XX (1928), 75. Two doubts were submitted to the Holy Office for solution.

I. Utrum in causis matrimonialibus acatholicus, sive baptizatus sive non baptizatus, actoris partes agere possit.

II. Utrum in quibuslibet causis matrimonialibus inter partem catholicam et partem acatholicam, sive baptizatam sive non baptizatam, quocumque modo ad Sanctam Sedem delatis, Suprema Sacra Congregatio Sanctii Officii exclusivam habeat competentiam.

To these doubts the Holy Office replied:

Ad I. *Negative*. seu standum Codici I.C., praesertim can. 87. Siquidem autem speciales occurrant rationes as admittendos acatholicos ut *actores* in huiusmodi causis, recurrendum ad Supremam Sacram Congregationem Sancti Officii in singulis casibus.

Ad II. *Affirmative*, habita praesertim ratione can. 247, §3, et salvo praescripto can. 1577, § 1, 1°.

all rightful standing in court. The resulting sentence, according to these authors, would be vitiated with irremediable nullity.[250] At times, however, there will exist a sufficient reason to justify the admission of an infidel as a plaintiff in an ecclesiastical court, and indeed in other than matrimonial causes. The law is clear and definite in reference to matrimonial causes when it demands that a proper authorization is to be secured from the Holy Office.[251] For example, if a pastor bought on credit some goods amounting to several hundred dollars, and then refused to pay the owner who happens to be unbaptized, justice and equity would demand that the infidel be enabled to sue the cleric before an ecclesiastical judge, and this in virtue of the privilege of the forum.[252] The Code is silent on the question of the infidel prosecuting an ecclesiastical suit in consequence of any acknowledged rightful standing in court. Certainly there would be no need to secure the permission of the Holy Office in such an event, since the Holy Office's permission is required specifically only for matrimonial causes.[253] The writer, therefore, holds the opinion that infidels have a standing in court in such causes altogether apart from the need of any permission. In matrimonial causes, however, the permission of the Holy Office must be secured.[254]

If the infidel person accepts a lawful summons as a defendant

[250] Cf. canons 87; 1646; Cappello, "De Acatholicorum Incapacitate," p. 400; Roberti, *De Processibus*, I, (2. ed.) nn. 198, 231; Doheny, *Canonical Procedure*, I, 115, 129.

[251] S.C.S. Off. resp. 27 ian. 1928 — *AAS*, XX (1928), 75; 22 mart. 1939— *AAS*, XXXI (1939), 131.

[252] The privilege of the forum means that the clergy and religious can be summoned as defendants only before the ecclesiastical judges to the exclusion of the civil courts, whether the case is contentious or criminal, unless the ordinary's consent be obtained either in individual causes, or as a general norm for particular places. — Cf. canon 120.

[253] Roberti, however, holds that the permission of the Holy Office is required for all causes if non-Catholics are involved. — *Apollinaris*, I (1928), 217. The writer does not agree with Roberti's opinion, for the Holy Office is concerned with questions touching faith and morals as such, and not with the question whether non-Catholics, as long as a matrimonial cause is not involved, may sue in court. — Canon 247.

[254] Non-Catholics are not estopped from acting as plaintiffs in the summary causes delineated in canon 1990. Permission to act is not required in

in a cause, the resulting sentence of such a trial would be valid. Noone states that a defendant who is lawfully summoned has the obligation to respond according to canon 1647.[255] The writer disagrees with this general statement of Noone. Infidels are not directly subject to the power of the Church and have no such obligation to respond, unless they become indirectly subject to the Church, e.g., through their relationship with persons or through some attendant connection with a cause which belongs to the Church as a spiritual matter.[256]

Baptized non-Catholics are not directly denied the right of a standing in court. The Code does not exclude non-Catholics as such from entering a suit (*ab agendo*). Moreover, the law before the Code admitted non-Catholics both as plaintiffs and as defendants in the causes that involved mixed marriages.[257] Also because of the silence of the Code there seems to be no reason today why the interpretation of the old law should be receded from, since the correction of law is always an odious matter.[258] Inasmuch as there are some authors[259] who exclude them on the ground that they are excommunicated,[260] it must be noted that non-Catholics as such are not *vitandi*, nor are they *tolerati* after a declaratory or a condemnatory sentence, and therefore are generally acknowledged a standing in court, in accord with canon 1654, §2.[261]

It should be noted that some authors admit that non-Catholics have some rightful standing in court in ecclesiastical trials.[262]

these causes. — Gasparri, *Tractatus Canonicus de Matrimonio* (ed. nova ad mentem Codicis I.C., 2 vols., Typis Polyglottis Vaticanis, 1932), II, n. 1260.

[255] Cf. *Nullity in Judicial Acts*, p. 51.

[256] Cf. Ottaviani, *Institutiones Iuris Publici Ecclesiastici*, I, n. 160; Bourque, *The Judicial Power of the Church*, p. 124.

[257] Cf. Wernz, *Ius Decretalium*, V, n. 169.

[258] Cf. Cappello, "De Acatholicorum Incapacitate," p. 398.

[259] Cf. Blat, *Commentarium*, Lib. IV, *De Processibus*, n. 122; Augustine, *A Commentary on the New Code of Canon Law* (8 vols., Vol. VII, 3. ed. St. Louis, Mo.: B. Herder and Co., 1930), VII, 106.

[260] Cf. canon 2314.

[261] Canon 1654, § 2: "Alii excommunicati generatim stare in iudicio queunt."

[262] Wernz-Vidal, *Ius Canonicum*, VI, n. 210; Cappello, "De Acatholicorum Incapacitate," p. 398; Coronata, *Institutiones Canonici Iuris*, III, n. 1173.

There are still other authors who deny this right to non-Catholics because of the response of the Holy Office.[263] The Holy Office declared in these responses that non-Catholics, whether baptized or unbaptized, are unable to act as plaintiffs in matrimonial causes, unless the proper authorization of the Holy Office is secured, and that the provisions of canon 87 are to be observed.[264] Noone states that this response refers directly to the right to impugn the validity of a marriage. He declares further that in virtue of its allusion to canon 87 it can be interpreted to refer to any type of judicial petition.[265] It is true that to the Holy Office has been reserved the right to permit non-Catholics to act is plaintiffs in matrimonial causes. There is no dispute on this point. The writer, however, takes exception to Noone's generalization that the response of the Holy Office refers to any type of judicial petition in view simply of the explicit mention of canon 87.[266] The two doubts proposed to the Holy Office were concerned only with matrimonial causes. The first doubt that was submitted concerned what is now under discussion. When asked whether in matrimonial causes non-Catholics, whether baptized or unbaptized, could act as plaintiffs (*actoris partes agere possit*), the Holy Office responded in the negative.[267] The Holy Office treated only of matrimonical causes, and decreed nothing else. In fact the Code declares that laws which decree a penalty, or restrict the free exercise of one's rights, or establish an exception to the law, must be strictly interpreted.[268] The writer believes

[263] S.C.S. Off., resp. 27 ian. 1928 — *AAS*, XX (1928), 75; also 22 mart. 1939 — *AAS*, XXXI (1939), 131; cf. Doheny, *Canonical Procedure*, I, 115; Cappello, "De Acatholicorum Incapacitate," p. 400.

[264] The Holy Office likewise declared that apostates are estopped from acting as plaintiffs in matrimonial causes — S.C.S. Off., resp. 15 ian. 1940— *AAS*, XXXII (1940), 52.

[265] Cf. *Nullity in Judicial Acts*, pp. 68-69.

[266] Cf. *supra*, footnote on page 82.

[267] The response: "Ad I. *Negative*, seu standum Codici I.C., praesertim can. 87. Siquidem autem speciales occurrant rationes ad admittendos acatholicos ut *actores* in huiusmodi causis, recurrendum ad Supremam Sacram Congregationem Sanctii Officii in singulis casibus. — S.C.S., Off., 27 ian. 1928 — *AAS*, XX (1928), 75.

[268] Cf. canon 19.

that the response of the Holy Office speaks for itself. If should not be extended to other judicial causes.

There are some authors[269] who feel that, if non-Catholics acted as plaintiffs in such causes without the permission of the Holy Office, the resulting sentence would be vitiated with irremediable nullity. The response of the Holy Office does not indicate such a conclusion. When the question was proposed to the Holy Office, the word "*possit*" was used. In the Matrimonial Instruction of 1936[270] the word "*nequeunt*" is employed. The use of these words, so it seems to the writer, does not imply invalidity for the act done in contravention of the law.[271]

The Pontifical Commission for the Authentic Interpretation of the Code has declared that atheists and guilty consorts are legally barred and disqualified from acting as plaintiffs in their marriage causes.[272] On January 4, 1946, however, the Pontifical Interpretation Commission declared that the estoppel of a guilty consort from impugning a marriage does not imply that the incapacity to enter a suit is of such a nature that the sentence is vitiated with the irremediable nullity mentioned in canon 1892, 2°.[273]

In the light of the response of the Pontifical Interpretation Committee to this question, which is analogous to the question of non-Catholics acting as plaintiffs, the writer agrees with Noone when he cautions that it is prudent to refrain from declaring the debarment of non-Catholics under sanction of invalidity of the sentence.[274]

[269] Cf. Doheny, *Canonical Procedure*, I, 115; Cappello, "De Acatholicorum Incapacitate," p. 400.

[270] *Instruction*, art. 35, § 3 — *AAS*, XXVIII (1936), 321.

[271] Cf. canon 11; cf. also Michiels, *Normae Generales Iuris Canonici* (2 vols., Dublin, 1929), II, 276, footnote 1. It is doubtful whether this "*non potest*" equivalently indicates the will of the legislator of voiding or incapacitating. This form seems ambiguous. Ordinarily, lawfulness is concerned; in doubtful cases only a prohibition is to be inferred from the use of such an expression.

[272] 17 jul. 1933 — *AAS*, XXV (1933), 345; 30 jul. 1934 — *AAS*, XXVI (1934), 494; 27 iul. 1942 — *AAS*, XXXIV (1942), 241.

[273] *AAS*, XXXVIII, (1946), 162.

[274] Cf. Noone, *Nullity in Judicial Acts*, p. 69.

Article 4. Unauthorized Procurators

Canon 1892. *Sentenria vitio insanabilis nullitatis laborat. quando: 3°. Quis nomine alterius egit sine legitimo mandato.*

A procurator is an agent properly appointed by a party and admitted by the ecclesiastical court for the purpose of representing the party before that tribunal.[275] The all-important provision concerning the procurator's mandate is that the judge shall not admit the procurator to plead until he has deposited in court a special written mandate of the party to represent him in the litigation. If this legitimate mandate is lacking, the sentence of the trial is vitiated with irremediable nullity.[276] A general mandate for a procurator is not sufficient; a specal mandate is needed for a procurator *ad litem*.[277]

Specification of the mandate does not imply that it must be determined in regard to a particular process. The judicial mandate may be special for one, for several, or for all causes.[278] In fact, the party may appoint such a procurator for just certain procedural acts, or for a single act.[279]

Another requisite for a legitimate mandate is that the mandate be granted in writing. The present legislation of the Code seems to do away with oral, tacit or presumed authorization.[280] A mandate which is not written would be illegitimate and in consequence of it the sentence would be irremediably null.[281]

[275] Cf. Hogan, *Judicial Advocates and Procurators*, The Catholic University of America Canon Law Studies, n. 133 (Washington, D.C.: The Catholic University of America Press, 1941), p. 4.

[276] Cf. canon 1659, § 1; 1892, 3°.

[277] Cf. Roberti, *De Processibus*, I, (2. ed.) 214. Coronata declares: "Si tamen mandatum detur generali modo ad omnia negotia etiam iudicialia, sufficere videtur etiam pro litibus." — *Institutiones Iuris Canonici*, III, n. 1185.

[278] Cf. Hogan, *Judicial Advocates and Procurators*, p. 103; Lega, *Commentarius*, I, 341.

[279] Cf. Roberti, *De Processibus*, I, (2. ed.) 212.

[280] Cf. canon 1659, § 1; Noval, *De Iudiciis*, n. 180; Roberti, *op. cit.*, I, (2. ed.) 214.

[281] Cf. canon 1892, 3°. Canon 1659, § 1: "... mandatum ad lites scriptum."

Canon 1659, §1, states further that the mandate of the defendant may even be given at the foot of the summons.[282] It seems sufficient if the opposing party is informed in the official citation of the fact that the plaintiff intends to act through a particular procurator.[283] The signature of the principal who grants authority to the procurator is necessary on the mandate, and the absence of this signature would cause the resulting sentence to be irremediably null.[284] The Matrimonial Instruction of 1936 further provides that the signature be certified by the pastor or by the notary of the curia.[285] This regulation is undoubtedly due to the fact that in recent years imposters have claimed the powers of a procurator and then have caused untold difficulties in certain suits at court. The proper certification of documents is particularly necessary when the parties are not known personally, and in the courts of quasi-domicile.[286] Further, the date and place with regard to the mandate's execution must be specified and a notation of these is required for the legitimacy of the mandate.[287] The document is to contain the name of the place wherein it is signed and must indicate the day, the month, and the year in which

[282] Canon 1659, §1: "... mandatum ... etiam in calce ipsius citationis." Hogan states that one may be inclined to believe that the citation proceeds from the *mandans*, whereas it derives from the judge. A lack of precision arises from the absence of a link referring the mandate to the citation, with the result that the clause would be clarified were it changed to read: *notatum etiam in calce ipsius citationis*. — *Op. cit.*, p. 105.

[283] Cf. Coronata, *Institutiones Iuris Canonici*, III, n. 1185, n. 5. The mandate is not illegitimate if this notification is not made, for the mandate is already executed. — Noone, *Nullity in Judicial Acts*, p. 73.

[284] Cf. canon 1659, § 1; Noval, *De Iudiciis*, n. 180.

[285] Article 49, § 1 — *AAS*, XXVIII (1936), 324. The Code itself does not require an official authentification of the principal's signature. — Roberti, *De Processibus*, I, (2. ed.) n. 214.

[286] Doheny, *Canonical Procedure*, I, 171. This certification, at least with reference to matrimonial procedure, seems to be required for the legitimacy of the mandate. — Hogan, *op. cit.*, pp. 105-106. The writer disagrees with this statement of Hogan, since the Code does not require an official authentication of the principal's signature. Canon 1892, 3°, is not involved, and consequently this certification is not required for the legitimacy of the mandate.

[287] Cf. canons 1659, § 1; 1892, 3°.

the principal affixed his signature.[288] If these requirements are lacking, the mandate is considered as illegitimate, and the sentence concluding the trial would be vitiated with irremediable nullity.[289] It must be noted that such documents have no force of proof in court, unless they are exhibited either in the original or in an authenticated copy and are deposited with the chancery of the court.[290]

If the person who issued the mandate does not know how to write, this must in the mandate be indicated in writing, and the pastor, or a notary of the curia, or two witnesses, shall sign the mandate in place of the person.[291] If for some reason, the principal is incapable of writing, then the mandate must under sanction of nullity also carry the announcement that the principal cannot affix his signature. In such a contingency the law demands an additional guarantee of the genuineness of the mandate. The guarantee referred to consists in the pastor's signature or in the signature of an ecclesiastical notary of the curia. If neither the pastor nor a diocesan notary signs the mandate, then two capable witnesses must sign in place of the principal for validity.[292] The mandate to the procurator must be preserved with the acts of the cause.[293]

This mandate of the procurator must be distinguished from the special mandate mentioned in canon 1662. A procurator needs a special mandate from the principal if he is to be given power to renounce the suit, or a prosecuting of the suit, or the judicial acts themselves. The procurator needs a special mandate if he is to make a friendly settlement or agreement with the other party, or before he can agree to have the case settled by arbitration. Moreover, the procurator needs a special mandate if he is to make an offer that his party will take an oath, or to ask the other party to take the oath.[294]

[288] Cf. canon 1659, § 1; cf. also Hogan, *op. cit.*, p. 107.

[289] Cf. canon 1892, 3°; Blat, *De Processibus*, n. 137.

[290] Canon 1819. Canon 1659, §1; ". . . mandatum . . . apud tribunal deposuerit."

[291] Canon 1659, § 2.

[292] Cf. Hogan, *Judicial Advocates and Procurators*, p. 108.

[293] Cf. canon 1660.

In regard to this special mandate, all the requirements and details as prescribed by canon 1659 must be observed under the sanction of irremediable nullity.[295]

Moreover, the procurator cannot act validly in a trial for his party if his mandate has come to an end, or if the mandate never existed in the first place.[296]

The mandate of the procurator is an important affair in judicial trials. If anyone acts in the name of another and completely lacks a mandate or one that is legitimate, the resulting sentence is vitiated with irremediable nullity.[297] The procurator's acts and the acts which the opposing party and the judge execute, in which the procurator must and does by law concur, are invalid; but the nullity of these acts does not nullify and void the other acts of the trial which preceded or followed, and which do not depend on the invalid acts.[298]

It may at this point be noted that the intent of the Code of Canon Law is to reduce, and not to increase, the number of invalid acts, invalid sentences and other forms of invalidity in matters pertaining to judicial procedure. The history of the *querela nulli-*

[294] Cf. canons 1662; 1746. The procurator does not need a special mandate either to prosecute the appeal, or to lodge a plaint of nullity against the sentence. — Cf. Hogan, *op. cit.*, pp. 111-115. A special mandate is needed for the extraordinary remedy of the plea for a *restitutio in integrum*. — Lega, *Commentarius*, I, (1950) 345. In reference to matrimonial causes, the Instruction of 1936 demands that the procurator have special authorization to represent the litigant in the court of the second instance. — Art. 52, § 2 — *AAS*, XXVIII (1936), 325. This is needed under the sanction of irremediable nullity, unless the original mandate specifically states that an authorization is given for both prosecutions or instances at court. — Cf. canons 1596; 1892, 3°.

[295] Cf. canon 1892, 3°. Blat, (*De Processibus*, n. 140) and Noval (*De Iudiciis*, n. 182) believe that the existence of a particular or of a general custom would prove sufficient to render obligatory a special mandate for certain judicial acts.

[296] Cf. Roberti, *De Processibus*, I, (2. ed.) n. 214. The procurator loses his mandate if he has effectively resigned from his commission, or has been removed from the cause when the party has made this removal known to the procurator. If, however, the issue of the trial has been joined, then this removal is not effective until it is made known to the judge and to the opposing party. — Canon 1664. Cf. also Roberti, *loc. cit.*

tatis contra sententiam, as discussed in Chapters I and II, indicates the same conclusion: only when essential elements are lacking or when the law plainly specifies an invalidating factor, as in canons 1892 and 1894, can nullity be proved or established.[299]

The advocate who is to undertake the prosecution of a cause must have from the party or from the judge a commission similar to the mandate of the procurator.[300] Unlike the procurator's mandate, the advocate's commission may derive either from the principal or from the judge of the trial. Consequently, the principal who wishes to avail himself of an advocate's legal assistance should so state in writing.[301] Though the commission of the advocate is to be similar to the mandate of the procurator, it does not follow that irremediable nullity is involved if such a commission is not similar to the procurator's mandate. Canon 1892, 3°, is concerned only with the lack of a mandate on the part of a person who is acting in the name of another person.[302]

In regard to the authorization of other legal representatives which was discussed above,[303] tutors and curators *ad litem* are appointed with a mandate of the legal authority as distinguished from the procurator *ad litem*, who generally receives his mandate from the party.[304] When canon 1892, 3°, decrees that whoever acts in the name of another must have a legitimate mandate under sanction of irremediable nullity, the law is concerned with the mandate of the procurator who is to act judicially in the name of another.[305] Consequently, the sentence is vitiated with irreme-

[297] Cf. canon 1892, 3°.

[298] Cf. canon 1680, § 2.

[299] Cf. canons 11; 1680; 1892; 1894.

[300] Cf. canon 1661.

[301] Cf. Coronata, *Institutiones Iuris Canonici*, III, n. 1186.

[302] Procurator pro parte et nomine partis ipse in iudicio stat; advocatus parti assistit. — cf. Coronata, *op. cit.*, III, n. 1179.

[303] Cf. *supra*, Article 3 of this Chapter, p. 66 ff.

[304] Differt procurator a curatore et tutore qui negotia agunt nomine alieno, non de mandato domini; sed vel de mandato iuris aut alius tertiae personae, e.g., iudicis. — Coronata, *Institutiones Iuris Canonici*, III, n. 1180.

[305] Cf. Pius IV (1559-1565), const. *In Throno Iustitiae*, 1561, § 13 — *Bull, Rom.*, VII, 155; const. *Cum ab Ipso*, 1562 — *Bull. Rom.* VII, 214; De Luca (1614-1683), *Theatrum Veritatis et Iustitiae*, VII, disc. 38, n. 22,

diable nullity only when the procurator acts in the name of another without a legitimate mandate. The proper remedy against such a sentence is the plaint of nullity by way either of a prosecuted suit or of a raised exception.[806]

p. 177; Schmalzgrueber, lib. II, tit. 1, n. 78. Cf. also modern authors — Coronata, *Institutiones Iuris Canonici*, III, n. 1418; Roberti, *De Processibus*, II, (1. ed.) n. 490.

[806] Cf. canons 1892, § 3°; 1893.

CHAPTER V

REMEDIABLE NULLITY OF THE SENTENCE

Canon 1894. *Sententia vitio sanabilis nullitatis laborat, quando:*

1°. *Legitima defuit citatio;*

2°. *Motivis seu rationibus decidendi est destituta, salvo praescripto can. 1605;*

3°. *Subscriptionibus caret iure praescriptis;*

4°. *Non refert indicationem anni, mensis, diei et loci quo prolata fuit.*

ARTICLE 1. THE JUDICIAL SUMMONS

Canon 1894. *Sententia vitio sanabilis nullitatis laborat, quando:* 1°. *Legitima defuit citatio.*

The bill of complaint or the oral petition having been admitted,[1] the other party must be summoned to appear in court. This summons issued by a court to the defendant is called the *vocatio in ius*.[2] Lemieux believes that the lack of the summons, as mentioned in canon 1894, 1°, is not concerned with the lack of the initial summons, but rather with the lack of the summons which should be issued when the sentence is to be published.[3] The writer, however, holds that canon 1894, 1°, refers only to the initial summons. This has been the accepted teaching of authors.[4] Moreover, the Rota has declared that canon 1894, 1°, is concerned with the initial summons.[5] The defendant has a right to a legitimate summons and the reception of a notice regarding the trial.

[1] Cf. canons 1706-1707.

[2] Cf. canon 1711, § 1; Coronata, *Institutiones Iuris Canonici*, III, n. 1240. The word "summons" denotes a formal command or citation, issued by the duly constituted authority of the tribunal, to have a person appear in court.

[3] Cf. *The Sentence in Ecclesiastical Procedure*, p. 89.

[4] Cf. Roberti, *De Processibus*, II, (1. ed.) n. 489; Noval, *De Iudiciis*, n. 661; Coronata, *Institutiones Iuris Canonici*, III, n. 1418.

[5] S.R.R., *Querela Nullitatis et Nullitatis Matrimonii*, 4 febr. 1939, coram R.P.D. Alberto Canestri, dec. X, n. 2 — *Decisiones*, XXXI, (1939), 85.

This right is founded on principles of the natural law.[6] The summons is to be sent to the defendant, and, if there are several defendants, to each one.[7] If the summons is not sent to all the defendants, then the defendants not summoned can insist that the procedural acts are null insofar as they are concerned.[8]

The Code of Canon Law demands certain elements in a judicial summons in order that the summons be legitimate. The summons is to be presented to the party in a written form, which shall express the precept of the judge to the party to appear.[9] This injunction of the judge is not merely an exhortation or a friendly invitation, as is the form of the summons for matrimonial causes of non-consummation, but rather a precept of the judge.[10] The summons would not be invalid, however, if the injunction of the judge was somewhat tempered.[11]

The mandate shall state the name of the judge who issues it.[12] This should include the complete name of the judge.[13] If a collegiate tribunal is to adjudicate the cause, the name of each of the judges should be indicated at the beginning of the summons, so that the defendant may see if any one of them be suspect.[14] Moreover, the better opinion cautions that a notice of the granted delegation be included in the summons if a delegated judge is to

[6] Cf. Lega, *Commentarius*, II, 525; Coronata, *Institutiones Iuris Canonici*, III, n. 1240.

[7] Cf. canon 1712; Coronata, *op. cit.*, III, n. 1242.

[8] Cf. canon 1894, 1°.

[9] Cf. canon 1715, § 1. Canon 1712 declares that the summons is to be written on the bill of complaint or joined to it. The Code does not demand that the bill of complaint itself be sent to the defendant, but this procedure would have its advantages. If the bill of complaint is not sent with the summons, this failure does not affect the legitimacy of the summons. — Coronata, *Institutiones Iuris Canonici*, III, n. 1241.

[10] Cf. Roberti, *De Processibus*, I (1. ed.), n. 290; *Regulae Servandae in Processibus super Matrimonio Rato et non Consummato*, 7 maii 1923, n. 36 — *AAS*, XV (1923), 389 ff.

[11] Cf. Roberti, *loc. cit.*

[12] Cf. canon 1715, §1.

[13] Coronata states: "Itemque necesse est ut eius nomen et cognomen, si fieri potest, designetur." — *Institutiones Iuris Canonici*, III, n. 1242.

[14] Cf. Coronata, *loc. cit.*; Roberti, *De Processibus*, I. (1. ed.) n. 290.

preside.[15]

The mandate must also indicate at least in general terms the reason why the party is summoned.[16] Since the Code demands only a general indication of the reason why the party is summoned, it is the lack of any indication whatsoever that alone will cause the summons to be invalid. One of the purposes of the summons is to let the defendant know why he has been summoned. Thus this requirement must be met.[17]

The summons must indicate the name and the surname of the defendant, and state also the name of the plaintiff.[18] The reason why the plaintiff's name is not to be omitted is that the defendant can know who is suing him. If it should happen that the judge does not know the name of the defendant, then the judge is to designate him by means of certain qualities or through mention of his office, so that the defendant can be perfectly identified.[19] If moral personalities or institutions such as colleges are to be summoned, it is sufficient to summon their administrators. If the defendant is a person who does not have the free administration of the goods concerned in the controversy, the summons must be presented to that person who in his name must answer in the trial.[20] The Pontifical Interpretation Commission has declared that, when a guardian has been assigned to a party, the summons is to be sent to the guardian, and not to the party for whom, as lacking the use of reason or as being weak-minded, he was legitimately assigned.[21]

[15] The Code does not require such a notice of the granted delegation, but authors recommend this procedure in order that there be afforded to the defendant an opportunity to investigate the jurisdiction of the judge. This omission does not cause invalidity. — Cf. Roberti, *loc. cit.*; Lega, *Commentarius*, II, 529.

[16] Cf. canon 1715, § 1.

[17] Cf. canon 1715, § 1; Roberti, *op. cit.*, I, (1. ed.) n. 291.

[18] Cf. canon 1715, § 1.

[19] Cf. Krol, *The Defendant in Contentious Trials*, p. 91. The Roman Rota declared a summons directed to the "Editors" null and void because it was not directed to specific persons. — S.R.R., *Treviren*, 15 naii 1913 — *AAS*, V (1913), 284.

[20] Cf. canon 1713; cf. also *supra*, Article 3 of this Chapter.

[21] Pont. Comm. Interp., 25 ian. 1943 — *AAS*, XXXV (1943), 58.

The summons is to contain a clear indication of the place where the defendant is to appear and of the time for this appearance, namely, the year, the month, the day, and the hour.[22] The place specified for the appearance of the defendant must be within the territory which is subject to the jurisdiction of the tribunal.[23] The judge cannot exercise judicial power outside his proper territory, except in the manner defined in canon 1637.[24] Canon 1636 states that the bishop can hold court at any place within his diocese with the exception of exempt places.[25] The time for the appearance of the defendant must be stated in the summons with mention of the year, the month, the day, and the hour.[26] The determining of the time for the defendant's appearance is discreti-

[22] Cf. canon 1715, § 1.

[23] Canon 1637 declares that a judge who has been expelled by force from his territory, or who is prevented from exercising jurisdiction there, may exercise his jurisdiction and pronounce sentence outside his territory. The judge, however, must inform the local ordinary that court is being held in his diocese. The omission of this notice to the local ordinary does not affect the validity of the procedure. — Roberti, *De Processibus,* I, (2. ed.) n. 167.

[24] Cf. canon 201, § 2. Noval stated that, if a judge does exercise judicial power outside his territory in circumstances other than those defined in canon 1637, such acts are illicit but not invalid. He based his opinion on the absence of an invalidating clause in canon 201, § 2 (*De Iudiciis,* n. 232). Roberti and all other authors hold that such acts of jurisdiction when performed outside of the proper territory would be invalid (*De Processibus,* I, (2. ed.) n. 167). The writer agrees with this latter view, since the judge outside his territory lacks jurisdiction. This was the opinion held by all the pre-Code authors. Also canon 201, § 2, seems at least equivalently to state the nullity of such acts.

[25] The bishop has no judicial power in a prelacy or abbacy *nullius,* since these prelates have their own territory separate from any diocese. — Cf. canon 319. There is a *dubium iuris* whether or not the bishop has judicial power on the exempt property of religious. The writer agrees with the opinion that the property of exempt religious is still within the territory of the local ordinary, though not of it, and consequently the bishop acts validly. In view of the *dubium iuris* the presumption stands for validity, in accorance with canon 209. — Cf. also Vermeersch-Creusen, *Epitome,* III, n. 71; Roberti, *De Processibus,* I, (2. ed.) n. 167.

[26] Canon 1715, § 1. Lega believes that an implied designation of the hour would be sufficient, especially when the bishop, in line with the ruling indicated in canon 1638, has fixed convenient hours during which access can be had to the court. — *Commentarius,* II, 530. The writer disagrees with this

onary with the judge, but the waiting period should be of sufficient length to enable the defendant to make the proper preparations. The length of the waiting period permitted does not affect the legitimacy of the summons, since this is not mentioned in the canon.[27]

Holy days of obligation and the last three days of Holy Week shall be observed as court holidays (*dies feriati*).[28] On these days it is forbidden to issue the summons, to hold court hearings, to examine the parties and the witnesses, to accept proofs, and to issue or execute decrees and sentences, unless necessity, Christian charity, or the public welfare demands that any of these things be undertaken.[29]

The last requirement for the written summons is that it must be authenticated with the seal of the court and subscribed by the judge or by his auditor and a notary.[30]

If the summons does not contain mention of the points enumerated in canon 1715, both the summons and the acts of the procedure are null and void.[31] It is to be noted that the summons is to be made in duplicate, one copy being presented to the defendant and the other inserted into the acts of the cause.[32]

The summons must be legally served if it is to produce juridical effects. There are three methods of serving the summons according to the Code: by courier, mail, and edict.[33]

The written summons is to be handed to the defendant per-

view. An indication of the time for the defendant's appearance is required under the sanction of invalidity, as is to be inferred from canon 1715, § 1.

[27] Cf. canon 1715, § 1.

[28] Cf. canons 1247, § 1; 1639, § 1.

[29] Canon 1639 does not invalidate the acts performed on these days, and states further that the judge is to decide and announce whether and which judicial acts are to be performed on these days.

[30] Cf. canon 1715, § 2. The signatures here referred to must be the living signatures of the judge or his auditor and the notary. The typed signature or the signature made by a rubber stamp is not sufficient, because someone else could readily enough forge the signatures of the judges and the notary.

[31] Cf. canons 1723; 1894, 1°.

[32] Canon 1716. According to canon 1712, if there are several defendants, each must receive a summons.

[33] Cf. canons 1717, § 1; 1719; 1720.

sonally by a messenger of the curia wheresoever the latter finds him, if this manner of serving the summons is possible.[34] The messenger may for this purpose enter the territory of another diocese, if the judge thinks it advisable and orders the messenger to do so.[35]

If the messenger does not find the person who is to be summoned in the place of his residence, he can leave the written summons with some person of the family or with a servant of the defendant, provided that such person is willing to receive it, and promises to give it to the defendant without delay.[36] Otherwise, as canon 1717, §2, states, the messenger shall take the summons back to the judge, in order that he may dispatch the summons in some other manner, as provided in the Code.[37]

If for reasons of distance or other factors it is difficult to have the summons delivered to the defendant by messenger, the judge

[34] Cf. canon 1717, § 1. These messengers shall be constituted either for all trials generally or for an individual cause. Cf. also canons 1591; 1592.

[35] Cf. canon 1717, § 2. Hanssen ("De sanctione nullitatis," *Apollinaris*, XI, [1938], 390) states that an implicit order of the judge is necessary for the valid service of the summons in another jurisdiction. Blat, (*De Processibus*, n. 213) declares that the order of the judge is merely a condition for the liceity of service. Lega (*Commentarius*, II, 531) and Noval (*De Iudiciis*, n. 400) hold the opinion that the messenger may not enter another jurisdiction to deliver the summons unless he be ordered to do so by the judge. The writer agrees with this latter opinion because of canon 1723, which declares that the summons is null if not legitimately served, and canon 1717, which states what is necessary for legitimately serving the written summons.

[36] Cf. canon 1717, § 3. Roberti declares that relatives or servants must be of sound mind and also past the age of puberty (can. 1757, §1), in order to be properly qualified to testify to the defendant's having received the summons. — *De Processibus*, I, (2. ed.) n. 294. The writer is in agreement with Roberti on this question.

[37] Lega (*Commentarius*, II, 532, 533) believed that the summons could be left with responsible neighbors (*ad vicinos*), and declared also that the summons could be affixed to the home of the defendant. The writer agrees with Krol when he states that such a method cannot be accepted, because such a method of summoning was not recognized prior to the Code as satisfying the demand of the law. Moreover, the codifiers did not adopt the suggestion of leaving the summons with neighbors. — Cf. Roberti, *Schemata*, F. c. 185, 4, n. 13, pp. 212-213. Canon 1717, § 3, gives the messenger no discretionary powers in this matter. — Cf. *The Defendant in Contentious Trials*, p. 93.

can order that it be transmitted by registered mail and that a signed receipt be obtained.[38] The judge may order that the summons be delivered to the defendant in any other manner which according to the laws and conditions of the country is considered the very safest.[39] Since the method of serving the summons by mail can be employed whenever it is difficult to serve the summons by messenger, there is no question of invalidity for lack of a sufficient reason when this method is used.[40]

Whenever after diligent inquiry the defendant still cannot be located, then the summons by edict or public announcement can be utilized.[41] Summons by edict is effected when the messenger posts the document of the summons at the doors of the curia in the manner of a public notice, which is to be left there for a length of time to be specified by the judge, and when the summons is also inserted in some newspaper or periodical. If not both of these means can be employed, then either manner of public notice proves sufficient.[42] It seems to the writer that the posting of the summons in the curial doors would receive but scant notice in most cities in the United States; accordingly the judge should also publish the summons in some public paper.[43] The Code does not determine the period of time which should elapse between the publishing of the summons by edict and the appearance of the defendant. This period of time is left to the judgment of the judge.[44] Nor does the Code state how often the summons

[38] Cf. canon 1719. This method of service is not an alternative one, but is to be employed only if it is difficult to have the summons delivered by messenger. For validity, the judge is to give an order for this method to be used; at least an implicit order of the judge would save the summons from invalidity. — Cf. canons 1719; 1723.

[39] Cf. canon 1719. "Alii modi transmittendi . . . transmissio per cursorem tribunalis laicalis, transmissio per curiam dioecesis in qua reus commoratur; itemque transmissio per parochum." — Coronata, *Institutiones Iuris Canonici*, III, n. 1246. Cf. also Roberti, *De Processibus*, I (1. ed.) n. 294.

[40] Cf. Coronata, *loc. cit.*; Noone, *Nullity in Judicial Acts*, p. 90.

[41] Cf. canon 1720, § 1.

[42] Cf. canon 1720, § 2.

[43] Lega believes that the former means would be certainly inefficacious. — *Commentarius*, II, 535.

[44] The practice of the Rota appears to be that the summons generally ap-

is to be published in the newspaper. The writer believes that even a single publication in a public paper would insure the legitimacy of the summons. Under ordinary circumstances, the diocesan paper should be used for this type of summons.[45]

Summons by edict is resorted to only when summons by messenger or by registered mail is impossible, since the former method is employed only when the actual whereabouts of a party remains unknown after diligent inquiry.[46] Certainly summons by edict can be ineffectual and should be employed only in exceptional cases.

If the summons was not legitimately served according to what has been discussed above, then the summons, the acts of the procedure, and the sentence are null.[47]

If the defendant appears before the judge of his own accord to please his cause, it is not necessary to issue the summons at all, but the notary should make note in the acts of the cause that the defendant came to court of his own accord.[48] If the defendant of his own accord appears in court, an invalid summons is thereby sanated; but if the party appears not of his own accord but only because he mistakenly thinks the summons to be legitimate, then the acts of the process and the sentence are remediably null.[49]

The provisions of canon 1721 in regard to the messenger's marking the date and the hour at which he handed the summons to the

pears in the *Acta Apostolicae Sedis* about two months before the date assigned for appearance. — *AAS*, XV (1923), 186. Article 68 of the *Normae S.R. Rotae Tribunalis* (*AAS*, XXVI [1934], 468) decrees: "tempore congruo assignato, ut ad notitiam rei conventi pervenire possit." Doheny (*Canonical Procedure*, I, 257) believes that, in the absence of a definite norm of law, a period of approximately three weeks should be of sufficient length for causes heard in a diocesan court.

[45] There is no prohibition against employing other papers with wider circulation, provided that there is no scandal nor any difficulty with the civil law. — Cf. Doheny, *loc. cit.*

[46] Cf. canon 1720.

[47] Cf. canons 1723; 1894, 1°.

[48] Cf. canon 1711, § 2.

[49] Cf. canons 1711, § 2; 1723. Cf. also Roberti, *De Processibus*, I, (1. ed.) n. 288; Noone, *Nullity in Judicial Acts*, p. 82.

defendant or his relatives, or at which he returned to summons to the judge, are not binding under the sanction of nullity.[50]

Lega maintained that the requirements of canon 1715 regarding the issuing of the summons are met if the requirements are substantially fulfilled. This opinion could engender troublesome consequences.[51] Canon 1723, indeed, states nothing concerning the substantial fulfillment of the requirements, but rather exacts under a sanction of nullity a full compliance with what canon 1715 prescribes.

If the defendant does not comply with the summons and offers no just excuse, he may be declared guilty of contempt of court.[52] The judge, however, cannot proceed to declare the party guilty of contempt unless the judge has first ascertained that the summons was legitimately issued and came to the notice of the defendant within due time, or at least should have come to him and that the defendant has neglected to offer an explanation for not appearing, or has given no valid excuse.[53]

The rules that have been discussed above for the summoning of the defendant shall be observed also in the other judicial acts, after they have been adapted to the diverse nature of these acts, such as in notifying the parties of the orders and sentences of the judge, in summoning witnesses, etc.[54] There is no question, however, of invalidity as it is mentioned in canon 1894, 1°, for the Code allows such rules for the summoning of the defendant to be adapted and applied according to the diverse acts of the judicial process.

[50] Coronata believes that these provisions are necessary under the sanction of nullity. — *Institutiones Iuris Canonici*, III, n. 1248. Canon 1723 decrees that the summons is null if it is not legitimately served. The provisions of canon 1721 are concerned only with the acts that follow upon the legitimate serving of the summons. The writer, therefore, does not agree with the opinion of Coronata. The same arguments hold as to the provisions of canon 1722 concerning the written report of his work which the messenger renders to the judge.

[51] Cf. *Commentarius*, II, 539.

[52] Cf. canon 1842. Every summons is peremptory. — Canon 1714.

[53] Cf. canon 1843, § 1. In order to declare the party guilty of contempt, the judge must follow the provisions of canons 1729, § 1, and 1842-1845.

[54] Cf. canon 1724.

In regard to the summoning of the plaintiff, the Code states that the plaintiff is to be notified by the court to appear on a specific day and at a fixed hour before the judge. The law does not demand any determined form for the summons of the plaintiff.[55] If the plaintiff is not notified and the joinder of issue is held without him, such a procedure would certainly result in invalidity, but not the invalidity against which the plaint of nullity could be employed. Canon 1894, 1°, is concerned only with the lack of the defendant's judicial summons.[56]

Though the Code does not state in express terms that the summons is necessary in the court of second instance, this does not mean that the summons is unnecessary. On the contrary, the court of second instance is to follow the same rules, accommodated to the matter in hand (*accommodatae ad rem*), as is the court of first instance.[57] The law requires a new joinder of issue in the court of second instance.[58] A new joinder of issue presupposes, therefore, that the defendant has been issued a legitimate summons.[59] If the summons in the court of second instance does not contain all the data and factors required in canon 1715, or if the summons has not been legitimately served, the summons and the processual acts are null, and the resulting sentence is vitiated with remediable nullity.[60]

Article 2. Statement of Motives

Canon 1894. *Sententia vitio sanabilis nullitatis laborat, quando, 2° Motivis seu rationibus decidendi est destituta, salvo praescripto can. 1605.*

[55] Cf. canon 1712, § 3.

[56] Cf. Roberti, *De Processibus*, II, n. 489; Coronata, *Institutiones Iuris Canonici*, III, n. 1418.

[57] Cf. canon 1595.

[58] Cf. canon 1891, § 1.

[59] Cf. *Querela Nullitatis et Nullitatis Matrimonii*, 10 aug. 1929, coram Massimi, dec. L, n. 2 — *Decisiones*, XXI (1937), 428.

[60] Cf. canons 1723; 1894, 1°.

The Code declares that, when the sentence[61] is issued, it must contain the reasons or the motives in fact and in law upon which the disposition of the controversy is made.[62] The sentence does not assume validity from the motives, but an exposition of the motives aids in the proper administration of justice, tends to confirm the belief of the parties in the justice of the sentence, and fosters jurisprudence.[63]

The general and particular laws, as also the juridical principles and the teachings which canonists use for solving the controversy proposed by the parties, are motives *in iure*. When these motives *in iure* are applied to the facts as described in the bill of complaint and actually proved in the course of the trial, then motives *in facto* arise.[64] The reasons, then, why the provisions of the law are applied in a particular way to the cause gives rise to the motives *in facto*.

The motives *in facto* amd *in iure* must be indicated in the sentence; otherwise the sentence is remediably null.[65]

The exception to the rule of law which demands the motives *in iure* and *in facto* is stated in canon 1605, namely the sentences of the Supreme Tribunal of the Apostolic Signatura are effective, even though they do not contain mention of the reasons in fact or in law.[66] Nevertheless, at the request of either party to the trial or, if it seems advisable, *ex officio*, this Supreme Tribunal may direct that the reasons for the sentence be published according to the proper regulations of this Tribunal.[67]

The judge is free to select those provisions of law which he deems applicable to the cause. He is not bound to follow the

[61] Canon 1868, § 1: Legitima pronuntiatio qua iudex causam a litigantibus propositam et iudiciali modo pertractatam definit, sententia est: eaque interlocutoria dicitur, si dirimat incidentem causam; definitiva, si principalem.

[62] Cf. canon 1873, § 1, 3°.

[63] Cf. Roberti, *De Processibus*, II, n. 456.

[64] Cf. Coronata, *Institutiones Iuris Canonici*, III, n. 1403.

[65] Cf. canon 1894, 2°. Cf. also *Lex propria S.R. Rotae et Signaturae Ap.*, 29 iun. 1908, c. 32, § 3 — *AAS*, I (1909), 29; *Regulae servandae in iudiciis apud S.R. Rota Tribunal*, 4 aug. 1910, § 182 — *Fontes*, n. 6461.

[66] Cf. canon 1605, § 1.

[67] Cf. canon 1605, § 2. Cf. also *Lex propria S.R. Rotae et Signaturae Ap.*, 29 iun. 1908 — *AAS*, I (1909), 20-29.

conclusions which the parties may have offered. Moreover, the motives *in facto* are to be taken from the acts and proofs of the cause.[68] Each assertion must be motivated if it is to appear in the dispositive part of the sentence which settles the controversy. Likewise, motivation of some sort of the decision may be implicitly contained in another part of the same decision.[69] The judge cannot simply refer to parts of another sentence issued by him or by another judge, nor can he grant the conclusions of the parties, nor the arguments proposed at the judicial trial, but it is permitted to the judge to deduce his own arrangements from all these for his decision.[70] The judge is not bound to follow each argument advanced by the attorneys; he not only can but he also must dispose of the points of controversy systematically.[71]

The judge is obliged to seek a true juridical basis for his judgment. He should not be unduly influenced by a lack of or an abundance of legal conclusions proposed by the parties.[72] The judge must also refer to and include the reasons for admitting or rejecting the testimony of the experts when he issues the sentence.[73] Canon 1894, 2°, is concerned only with the lack of motives *in iure* and *in facto*, and consequently the plaint of nullity would not avail for attacking a sentence which lacked the reasons for admitting or rejecting the testimony of the experts. If evident and certain error contrary to the provisions of substantive law is contained in the listing of the motives *in iure*, and also if an error is made in the reasons or motives *in facto*, such sentences are to be attacked by means of an appeal or with the plea for a *restitutio in integrum*, and not with the plaint of nullity. The reason for this statement is that canon 1894, 2°, is not involved, since the motives were stated, even though erroneously.[74]

When a controversy has been adjudicated by a collegiate tribunal, the recording judge (*relator*) is limited to the use of those

[68] Cf. Roberti, *De Processibus*, II, n. 456.

[69] Cf. canon 1873, § 1, 3°; Roberti, *loc. cit.*

[70] Cf. Lega, *Commentarius*, II, 959; Roberti, *loc. cit.*

[71] Cf. Roberti, *De Processibus*, II, n. 456.

[72] Cf. Wernz-Vidal, *Ius Canonicum*, VI, n. 592.

[73] Cf. canon 1804, § 2; Coronata, *Institutiones Iuris Canonici*, III, n. 1333.

[74] Cf. canon 1894. 2°: Coronata, *op. cit.*, III, n. 1403.

motives *in iure* and *in facto* which were proposed by the judges of the trial. The recording judge (*relator*) must state specific motives if the collegiate tribunal so orders.[75]

If false reasons or motives are given in the sentence, then the plaint of nullity against the sentence can be lodged, inasmuch as the presence only of false reasons can be equated with the absence of all reasons.[76]

The form of the sentence does not concern the discussion relating to the plaint of nullity against the sentence. Whether the motives *in facto* precede or follow the motives *in iure* is not a problem for this dissertation. Only the failure to indicate both the motives *in iure* and the motives *in facto* for the sentence gives rise to remediable nullity. Therefore, the reasons *in iure* and *in facto* must be given if the sentence is to be valid. If either the reasons *in iure* or the reasons *in facto* are omitted, the sentence is remediably null.[77]

Article 3. Signatures, Date and Place

Canon 1894. *Sententia vitio sanabilis nullitatis laborat, quando, 3°. Subscriptionibus caret iure praescriptis;*

4°. Non refert indicationem anni, mensis, diei et loci quo prolata fuit.

Another cause of remediable nullity in the sentence is the lack of the signatures which are demanded by the law. The sentence must be subscribed by the judge of the trial, or by all the judges if there are several, and by a notary.[78] If the sentence bears the signature of only one judge of a collegiate tribunal and the notary

[75] Cf. canon 1873, § 2; Roberti, *De Processibus*, II, n. 456. "Ponens seu relator est quasi iudex instructor in tribunalibus collegialibus; cui tamen non solum causae instructio, sed praeterea redactio in scriptis sententiarum committenda est" — Coronata, *Institutiones Iuris Canonici*, III, n. 1122.

[76] Cf. Doheny, *Canonical Procedure*, I, 517.

[77] Cf. canon 1894, 2°.

[78] Cf. canon 1874, § 5. By the term "signature" is understood the act of putting down one's name at the end of an instrument to attest its validity.—*Bouvier's Law Dictionary* (Baldwin's ed., Banks-Baldwin Law Pub., 1946). By signature then is meant the name of any person, written with his own hand.

of the court, the resulting sentence would be invalid.[79] The writer agrees with Doheny[80] when he states that it is not necessary that the judges of a collegiate tribunal affix their signatures in the presence of one another. The Code does not demand this. It must also be noted that if one or more of the judges of a collegiate tribunal inadvertently forget to sign the sentence, this oversight can be corrected and the sentence rectified by way of a simple supplying of the missing signatures, provided this is done within three months from the publication of the sentence, and a plaint of nullity has not been lodged against the sentence.[81]

It seems to the writer than when the law demands the signatures of the judges and of the notary, it is not necessary for validity that the complete name be given. It would be sufficient to indicate the family name. The complete name, however, of the judge and of the notary should ordinarily be used. It is not sufficient for the judges and the notary merely to use initials when signing the sentence.[82]

The signature of the notary is necessary as a public attestation of the authenticity of the signatures of the judges, since the notary is considered as a specifically accredited witness (*testis qualificatus*) in the Code.[83] Therefore, by means of his own signature at the end the judicial notary attests to the genuineness of the signatures of the judges. The notary should be present at the signing of each judge.[84] If the signature of the subscriber is not legible, or if some doubt arises concerning the identity of the person signing the sentence, all possible diligence is to be employed to settle the doubt.[85] If the doubt cannot be settled in a manner

[79] Cf. canon 1894, 3°; Pont. Comm. Interpr., 14 iul. 1922 — *AAS*, XIV (1922), 529.

[80] Cf. *Canonical Procedure*, I, 517.

[81] Cf. Doheny, *loc. cit.*; cf. also canons 1895; 1897, § 2.

[82] Cf. "De Sanctione Nullitatis in Processu Canonico," *Apollinaris*, XII (1939), 235. The signatures of the judges and the notary must be the living signatures, and not such as are produced in some mechanical manner. Otherwise, the signatures could easily be forged.

[83] Cf. canons 1585, § 1; 1813, § 1.

[84] Cf. Duerr, *The Judicial Notary*, p. 81; Metz, *The Recording Judge in the Ecclesiastical Collegiate Tribunal*, p. 94.

[85] Cf. Lega, *Commentarius*, II, 1028.

that will indicate the nature of the signature or the identity of the subscriber, the plaint of nullity against the sentence is not made available, since canon 1894, 3°, is applicable only if the prescribed signatures are lacking. Therefore the question here revolves around signatures drawn in compliance with the law. The Code is silent concerning the seal of the tribunal. It is the opinion of the writer that from the Code's silence one may conclude that a failure to employ the seal does not cause the sentence to be invalid.[86]

The sentence of a trial is to close with mention of the date on which and the place in which it was framed.[87] The year, the month, the day, and the place must be indicated. These indications are all necessary for the validity of the sentence, and if the date or the place are not stated, the sentence is vitiated with remediable nullity.[88]

Although canon 1874, §5, states that the sentence shall conclude with mention of the date on which and of the place in which it was framed, canon 1894, 4°, decrees only that the sentence, under sanction of remediable nullity, bear mention of the year, the month, the day and the place of its framing; it decrees nothing to the effect that the sentence is to conclude with these indications.[89] It is the opinion of the writer that if the time and the place are indicated at the beginning of the sentence, there is no necessity of a repetition of this at the close of the sentence. The sentence would not be invalid under such conditions.[90]

[86] Cf. Doheny, *Canonical Procedure*, I, 518; Roberti, *De Processibus*, II, n. 489.

[87] Cf. canon 1874, § 5.

[88] Canon 1894, 4°. Doheny states that the complete date and the precise locality must be indicated with exactitude, otherwise the sentence is invalid.— *Canonical Procedure*, I, 518.

[89] Canon 1894: Sententia vitio sanabilis nullitatis laboret, quando: 4°. Non refert indicationem anni, mensis, diei et loci quo prolata fuit.

[90] Lega declared that if the year and the place are indicated in the text of the sentence, and only the month and the day are affixed at the bottom of the sentence, the resulting sentence is valid. — *Commentarius*, II, 1028. Lemieux states that if the date and the place are stated at the beginning of the sentence, they need not be repeated, as it suffices simply to indicate them

An interlocutory sentence ordinarily settles some incidental cause or point, but does not determine the principal controversy so as virtually to settle it. An interlocutory sentence, however, can have definitive force when it materially affects the main issue and in such a way as virtually to decide it.[91] The plaint of nullity can be lodged against an invalid interlocutory sentence which has definitive force, just as it can be employed against an invalid definitive sentence.[92] Since this is so, it follows that such an interlocutory sentence which has definitive force is to be dated and signed by all of the judges and the notary. The question is to be indicated briefly together with the reasons supporting the decision.[93] The plaint of nullity, therefore, does pertain to an interlocutory sentence if this sentence has definitive force and is vitiated with irremediable or remediable nullity.[94] The plaint of nullity against the sentence is not employed against a sentence which does not have definitive force, nor against the decrees of the judge, nor against the remaining processual acts. In these contingencies the process of nullity.[95] constitutes only a special

again, e.g., "Datum, die et loco supra dictis.—" *The Sentence in Ecclesiastical Procedure*, p. 86.

[91] Lemieux, *op. cit.*, p. 7; Vermeersch-Creusen, *Epitome*, III, n. 228; Coronata, *Institutiones Iuris Canonici*, III, n. 1394.

[92] Cf. Coronata, *op. cit.*, III, n. 1417.

[93] Cf. Lemieux, *The Sentence in Ecclesiastical Procedure*, pp. 87-88. Noval stated that the interlocutory sentence is to be signed by the judges and the notary and must indicate the date and the place. — *De Iudiciis*, n. 5630. Vermeersch-Creusen declare that the interlocutory sentence is to contain a brief narration of the issue and the conclusions of the parties, the motives, mention of the date and the place, and the signatures of the judges and the notary. — *Epitome*, III, n. 232. Coronata believes that the requirements of canon 1874 are not of strict obligation, though they should generally be observed for interlocutory sentences which have a definitive force. — *Institutiones*, III, n. 1402.

[94] Cf. canons 1892; 1894. Cf. also Coronata, *Institutiones Iuris Canonici*, III, n. 1417; *Regulae servandae in iudiciis apud Supremum Signaturae Ap. Tribunal*, 6 *mart.* 1912, art. 3 — *Fontes*, n. 6462.

[95] Canon 1679 declares that the party has a right to sue in court for the declaration of nullity of an act or a contract that is invalid by law. Such an action is not, however, to be confused with the *querela nullitatis contra sen-*

phase in the principal process. Generally, this process of nullity is handled as an incidental question.[96]

tentiam, which is applicable only to sentences vitiated with the types of nullity that receive mention in canons 1892 and 1894.

[96] Cf. Roberti, *De Processibus*, I (1. ed.) n. 241; II, n. 495.

CHAPTER VI

THE FUNCTION OF THE PLAINT OF NULLITY

Article 1. The Plaint of Nullity as an Exception

Canon 1893. *Nullitas de qua in can. 1892 proponi potest per modum exceptionis in perpetuum.*

By an exception, authors[1] mean an assertion of the defendant agianst some right until then recognized for, or some fact attributed to the plaintiff by which the latter's judicial action is delayed or estopped.[2] An exception truly supposes "that the plaintiff has a valid action, but due to some circumstance independent of the basis of the claim the action is liable to delay or complete nullification by virtue of an exception registered by the defendant."[3]

By placing an exception, the defendant actually becomes a plaintiff and calls into question the status of the original plaintiff in the case. It may be noted that the plaintiff seeks to establish his rights in court by means of his action; the defendant tries to exclude the action by means of the exception.[4]

Exceptions are classified as either peremptory or dilatory.[5] As an exception, the plaint of nullity against the sentence amounts to a peremptory exception, because it obstructs the judicial action of the plaintiff perpetually, or completely destroys his right to

[1] Cf. Noval, *De Iudiciis*, n. 293; Roberti, *De Processibus*, I, (1. ed.) n. 272; Coronata, *Institutiones Iuris Canonicis*, III, n. 1194.

[2] "Exceptio est assertio rei contra factum vel ius actoris, qua ipsius actio retardatur vel eliditur." — Coronata, *loc. cit.*

[3] Cf. Coyle, *Judicial Exceptions*, p. 2.

[4] Cf. Roberti, *De Processibus*, I, (1. ed.) n. 272; Noval *De Iudiciis*, nn. 298, 300; Lega, *Commentarius*, I, (1950) 358.

[5] Peremptory exceptions obstruct the judicial action of the plaintiff perpetually, or completely destroy his right to sue in a particular case. Dilatory exceptions are those which postpone the entering of a suit for a time, or delay the issue temporarily. — Cf. Coyle, *Judicial Exceptions*, pp. 3-4. Cf. also Coronata, *Institutiones Iuris Canonici*, III, n. 1195; Roberti, *op. cit.*, I, n. (1.ed.) 273; Noval, *op. cit.*, n. 299.

sue in a particular case. A peremptory exception destroys the right to sue, but allows the possibility of the consideration of the cause on its own merits.[6] An exception is by its nature a means of defense. The plaint of nullity as an exception, therefore, tends to this object: to oppose and estop the judge in the execution of the sentence, or to estop the victorious litigant in having enforced a sentence pronounced in his favor.[7]

A judicial exception is of its very nature perpetual.[8] The exception stands ever available and is of its very nature applicable as something permanently abiding and temporally unrestricted.[9] When the right to entering a suit has been forfeited, e.g., when legal prescription against the possible entering of a suit has run its full course, the right to raise an exception does not cease by prescription, nor in any other way in which the right to the entering of a suit may lapse.[10] The reason for this difference is that a plaintiff is free to enter a suit and may do so within a convenient time, while the defendant is not free to propose an exception but depends upon the will of his opponent.[11] Thus the defendant should and does have the right to protect himself against even an unjust aggressor who could easily employ the time element to his own advantage.[12]

Simple peremptory exceptions must be raised after the joinder of issue. Since these peremptory exceptions seek to rule out the prosecution of the judicial action on its objective merits, and since the action of the plaintiff is in its nature not determined until the joinder of issue, the procedure is to propose peremptory exceptions after the issue has been joined.[13]

The plaint of nullity as an exception remains available as an

[6] Cf. Coyle, *Judicial Exceptions*, p. 4.

[7] Cf. Lega, *Commentarius*, II, 1023; Coronata, *op. cit.*, III, n. 1417.

[8] Cf. canons 1667; 1698, § 2; 1893.

[9] Cf. Krol, *The Defendant in Contentious Trials*, p. 104.

[10] Cf. Lega, *Commentarius*, I, (1950) 360; Roberti, *De Processibus*, I (1. ed.) n. 275; Woywod, *A Practical Commentary on the Code of Canon Law*, II, n. 1637.

[11] Cf. Roberti, *loc. cit.*

[12] Cf. Noval, *De Iudiciis*, n. 301; Coyle, *Judicial Exceptions*, p. 8.

[13] Cf. canon 1629, § 2. Cf. also Coyle, *Judicial Exceptions*, p. 23; Coronata, *Institutiones Iuris Canonici*, III, n. 1156.

abiding remedy which can be invoked before any competent tribunal.[14] Canon 1893 declares that the plaint of nullity as a judicial action or suit against an irremediably null sentence is to be lodged only before the judge who issued the sentence, but this canon does not decree the same restriction for the plaint of nullity as an exception.

The plaint of nullity as an exception can be proposed against a sentence vitiated with irremediable nullity.[15] Whenever a sentence has been issued by a judge or by a collegiate tribunal absolutely incompetent, the exception can be proposed.[16] The plaint of nullity as an exception can also be lodged against any sentence issued by a tribunal which did not have the requisite number of judges demanded by canon 1576, §1.[17] The plaint of nullity as an exception can be proposed against a sentence which has been issued when at least one of the parties did not have any rightful standing in court.[18] Finally, the plaint of nullity as a judicial exception can be employed against a sentence when one has prosecuted the cause in the name of another person without the lawful mandate to do so.[19]

A problem arises concerning the employment of the plaint of nullity as an exception for the purpose of attacking a remediably invalid sentence. Coyle[20] maintains that the plaint of nullity as an exception remains inapplicable to remediable nullities. The reasons advanced by Coyle are the wording of canon 1893, which refers only to irremediable nullities, and also the fact that an exception, being of its nature perpetual, cannot have a place in regard to nullities that can be sanated within a time limit.

The writer does not agree with this opinion.[21] There is no con-

[14] Cf. canon 1667. Cf. also Reiffenstuel, lib. II, tit. XXVI, n. 66; Coronata, *op. cit.*, III, n. 1419; Doheny, *Canonical Procedure*, I, 515; Roberti, *De Processibus*, I, (1. ed.) n. 275.

[15] Cf. canon 1893.

[16] Cf. canons 1892, 1°; 1893. Cf. also *supra*, Chapter IV, Article 1.

[17] Cf. canons 1892, 1°; 1893. Cf. also *supra*, Chapter IV, Article 2.

[18] Cf. canons 1892, 2°; 1893. Cf. also *supra*, Chapter IV, Article 3.

[19] Cf. canons 1892, 3°; 1893. Cf. also *supra*, Chapter IV, Article 4.

[20] Cf. *Judicial Exceptions*, p. 55.

[21] Vermeersch-Creusen state that the exception can be joined with an

tradiction in employing the plaint of nullity as an exception to attack remediably invalid sentences. It must be noted that a party can defend his rights indirectly by means of exceptions.[22] Inasmuch as a judicial exception provides a legitimate means of defense, the writer maintains that a party has a right to employ the plaint of nullity as an exception in order to oppose and estop the judge in the execution of a remediably null sentence, or in order to estop the victorious litigant in making use of a remediably null sentence pronounced in his favor.

Even though an exception is of its nature considered perpetual,[23] there is no rule of law which states that the plaint of nullity as an exception cannot be employed during the time limit before the automatic sanation takes effect.[24]

When the plaint of nullity is proposed as a simple exception, the general norms which govern the hearing of incidental questions in a trial are to be followed, since no particular norms for any other procedure are set down in the Code.[25] The plaint of nullity is proposed by way of a judicial petition which is to contain the reasons for attacking the sentence. The opposing party should be notified, as well as the defender of the bond, if he has taken part in the cause. The promoter of justice should also be cited when the plaint of nullity is involved, because the public good is concerned.[26] The joinder of issue is to take place, at least informally. If the party who is lodging the exception fears, however, that the judge who, or the collegiate tribunal which pronounced the sentence is prejudiced, but intends to raise the exception in the same trial instance, he may demand that another judge or personnel of judges be substituted for the hearing of the ex-

appeal for the purpose of attacking a remediably null sentence. — *Epitome*, III, n. 242. Cf. also Blat, *De Processibus*, n. 428.

[22] Cf. canon 1667.

[23] Cf. canons 1667; 1698, § 2; 1893.

[24] Cf. canons 1894; 1895.

[25] Cf. canons 1837-1841. Cf. Wernz-Vidal, *Ius Canonicum*, VI, n. 620; Roberti, *De Processibus*, II, n. 500; Goyeneche, *De Processibus*, I (Romae: ad S. Ioannis Lat., pro manuscripto, 1950), p. 192.

[26] Cf. Roberti, *loc. cit.*; Coronata, *Institutiones Iuris Canonici*, III, n. 1419.

ception.[27] If the party invokes the provision of canon 1896, this must take place before the joinder of issue.[28] The procedure continues in the ordinary manner, and concludes with a sentence or a decree. The party has at his disposal all the remedies of law against this sentence or decree.[29] The plaint of nullity as an exception should be settled in as brief a manner as possible and with a minimum of delay because of the nature of the cause.[30]

When the exception is entered as an incidental question, the petition is to be treated as any other incidental question and settled according to canon 1840. The judge is to decide if it is to be defined by way of a decree, or if a full judicial form is to be observed because of the special type and gravity of the question.

The plaint of nullity as an exception is directed against the definitive sentence, and is a process which places in issue the validity of the sentence. If, however, all of the judicial acts are alleged to be null, the process will be a twofold one, the first concerning the nullity of the sentence, and the second, at the instance of the interested party, concerning the nullity of the acts. The nullity of the acts may entail a re-investigation and judgment on the merits of the cause.[31]

In regard to irremediable nullity, when are the acts of the cause likewise null so that there must be a double process?[32] When a sentence is declared null as a result of the absolute incompetence of the tribunal, all the acts of the cause and process are null.[33] The reason for this is that the judge has no jurisdiction if he is absolutely incompetent, and the situation is then of such a nature as if no trial had been held at all.[34] If, however, the sentence is declared null because of a lack of the legitimate number of judges, then

[27] Cf. canons 1896; 1615.

[28] Cf. canon 1628, § 1; Roberti, *De Processibus*, II, n. 500.

[29] Cf. canon 1840; Roberti, *loc. cit.*; Goyeneche, *De Processibus*, I, 193.

[30] Cf. Wernz-Vidal, *Ius Canonicum*, VI, n. 620.

[31] Cf. Roberti, *De Processibus*, II, nn. 495, 500; Goyeneche, *De Processibus*, I, 192.

[32] Cf. *infra*, Article 2 of this Chapter, p. 121, in regard to remediable nullity.

[33] Cf. Coronata, *Institutiones Iuris Canonici*, III, n. 1418; Goyeneche, *De Processibus*, I, 189.

[34] Cf. canon 1680, § 1.

only those acts are null which depend on or demand the presence of all the judges. Therefore only certain acts need to be repeated.[35]

If one of the parties lacked the right of appearing personally in court,[36] it seems to the writer that the entire process should be repeated, inasmuch as all the other acts of the cause depend on the fact that both parties must have a rightful standing in the court.[37] When someone has acted in the name of another without a legitimate mandate,[38] only those acts of the cause are null — and consequently must be repeated — which depend on the procurator, or also those acts of the judge and of the opposing party in which the procurator must concur. The reason for this statement is that the nullity of any one given act does not make null and void the acts which precede or follow, as long as these do not in any way depend on the invalid act.[39]

An irremediably invalid sentence cannot become sanated through the lapse of any given duration of time. There can be no appeal to the Rota or to the Holy Office. Doheny maintains that the only means of a sanation lies with the Apostolic Signatura.[40]

Article 2. The Plaint of Nullity as an Action

In this article, the plaint of nullity in its nature of a judicial action will be considered in two sections. First, it will be dis-

[35] Cf. canon 1680, § 2; Coronata, *loc. cit.* The full number of judges must determine the sentence. All those procedural acts which pertain to the drawing up of the acts of the cause and which can be committed to one who functions as the auditor do not demand the presence of the entire tribunal.—Roberti, *De Processibus*, I, n. 113; Lega, *Commentarius*, I, 134.

[36] Cf. canon 1892, 2°.

[37] Cf. canon 1680; Goyeneche, *De Processibus*, I, 189.

[38] Cf. canon 1892, 3°.

[39] Cf. canon 1680, § 2. Goyeneche maintains that in consequence of the irremediable nullity of the sentence the entire process is null, and consequently must be repeated. — *De Processibus*, I, 189.

[40] Cf. *Canonical Procedure*, I, 520. Doheny does not offer any proof for this statement. Canons 1602-1605 do not cover this procedure; in fact, there is no rule of law acknowledging such competence to the Signatura. The writer, therefore, is of the opinion that the Supreme Pontiff alone should be approached for the granting of such a sanation.

cussed as an action against a sentence vitiated with irremediable nullity, and secondly, as an action against a sentence vitiated with remediable nullity.

Section 1. Against Irremediably Invalid Sentences

Canon 1893. *Nullitas de qua in can. 1892 proponi potest . . . per modum vero actionis . . . intra triginta annos a die publicationis sententiae.*

The Code declares that every right can be enforced by means of an action in court, unless the contrary is explicitly stated.[41] The plaint of nullity against a sentence vitiated with irremediable nullity can be proposed as an action.[42]

Judicial action in contentious causes is either a proprietary suit (*actio petitoria*), or a possessory suit (*actio possessoria*). The former consists in the vindication or prosecution of one's right under the law, and the latter is an action to obtain the possession of an object, or the quasi-possession of a right, e.g., the unimpeded use and free exercise of one's rights.[43] The plaint of nullity against the sentence is to be classified as a proprietory action,[44] and therefore consists in the vindication or prosecution of one's right under the law to have the sentence set aside.

The plaint of nullity as an action is the proper remedy of law for attacking a sentence vitiated with irremediable nullity.[45] Therefore this action can be lodged against a sentence which has been issued by a judge who was absolutely incompetent,[46] or in a collegiate tribunal by an insufficient number of judges.[47] The action can also be employed against a sentence vitiated with irre-

[41] Cf. canon 1667. Canons 1017, § 3; 1971, § 1, 1°, and 1701 reflect possible examples of the exceptions mentioned in canon 1667.

[42] Actio est ius persequendi in iudicio quod nostrum est aut quod nobis debetur. — Coronata, *Institutiones Iuris Canonici*, III, n. 1192; Lega, *Commentarius*, I, 357.

[43] Cf. canon 1668.

[44] Cf. Lega, *Commentarius*, I, (1950) 356; Beste, *Introductio in Codicem*, p. 803.

[45] Cf. canon 1893.

[46] Cf. *supra*, Article I of Chapter IV.

[47] Cf. *supra*, Article 2 of Chapter IV.

mediable nullity when one of the parties lacked all rightful standing in the court,[48] or when someone has acted in the name of another without a legitimate mandate.[49]

When the plaint of nullity against the sentence is proposed as an action, the general norms which govern trials are to be followed, since no separate particular norms for procedure are set down in the Code.[50] The plaint of nullity against the sentence is proposed by means of a new judicial petition. This petition names the tribunal that is being called upon, delineates the sentence that is being attacked, and lists the reasons for attacking the sentence. When the petition has been admitted by the judge, the other party is to be notified. The promoter of justice is to be called in these causes, since the public good is always concerned in questions of nullity of the sentence.[51] Then follows the joinder of issue. Thereupon the procedure continues in the ordinary manner and concludes with a sentence. The party has at his disposal all the remedies of law against the sentence.[52] The plaint of nullity against the sentence should be settled in as brief a manner as possible.[53]

When the plaint of nullity as an action is lodged against the sentence, it is constituted as a new process, which has as its object a judicial pronouncement regarding the validity or the invalidity of the sentence.[54]

When a sentence has been declared irremediably null because of the absolute incompetence of the tribunal, the process is also null, and therefore must be repeated if there is to result a valid sentence on the merits of the cause.[55] The reason for this state-

[48] Cf. *supra,* Article 3 of Chapter IV.

[49] Cf. *supra,* Article 4 of Chapter IV.

[50] Cf. Roberti, *De Processibus,* II, n. 500.

[51] Cf. canon 1708; Roberti, *loc. cit.*; Coronata, *Institutiones Iuris Canonici,* III, n. 1419; Wernz-Vidal, *Ius Canonicum.* VI, n. 620; Goyeneche, *De Processibus,* I, 192.

[52] Cf. Roberti, *loc. cit.*; Goyeneche, *op. cit.,* I, 193.

[53] Cf. Wernz-Vidal, *loc. cit.*

[54] Cf. Roberti, *De Processibus,* II, n. 495; Goyeneche, *De Processibus,* p. 192.

[55] Cf. canon 1892, 1°; Coronata, *Institutiones Iuris Canonici,* III, n. 1418; Goyeneche, *ibid.,* p. 189.

ment is that an essential constituent is lacking in such a trial. All the other acts which, whether preceding or following, depend on the invalidity of the principal act are thereby rendered inefficacious.[56] If a sentence is declared irremediably null because of a lack of the legitimate number of judges, then only those acts are null which demanded the presence of the entire tribunal. Consequently, there is no need to renew all the acts of the cause.[57] If one of the parties lacked the right to appear personally in court, it seems to the writer that the entire process should be renewed inasmuch as all the acts of the cause depend on such essentials as those which relate to the right on the side of both of the parties to appear in court.[58] In regard to a procurator who has acted in the name of another without a legitimate mandate, only those acts of the cause are null which depend on the procurator or also on the acts of the judge or of the opposing party in which the procurator must concur.[59]

The plaint of nullity against an irremediably null sentence can be proposed as an action only within thirty years from the date of the publication of the sentence.[60] In the loss of rights, frequently the lapse of a predetermined or set period of time becomes an important factor. In contentious causes the actions or suits entered in court, whether real or personal, are extinguished through the operation of prescription according to the rules of canons

[56] Cf. canon 1680.

[57] Cf. canon 1680; 1892, 1°; Coronata, *loc. cit.* The entire collegiate tribunal must determine the sentence. All procedural acts which are concerned with the drawing up of the acts of the case and which can be committed to one who functions as the auditor do not demand the presence of all the judges. — Cf. Roberti, *De Processibus*, I, n. 113; Lega, *Commentarius*, I, (1950) 134.

[58] Cf. canons 1680; 1892, 2°.

[59] Cf. canons 1892, 3°; 1680.

[60] Cf. canon 1893. The publication of the sentence can be made in three ways: 1) through a summoning of the parties to hear the sentence solemnly read by the judge sitting in court; 2) through a notifying of the parties that the sentence is at the chancery of the court where they are authorized to read it and to obtain copies of it, or 3) through the sending of a copy of the sentence by registered mail, if locally that is the established practice — Canon 1877.

1508-1512. Judicial actions which deal with the status of persons, e.g., with the validity of their religious profession, or their sacred orders, or of their marriage, never become extinguished.[61] These canons, i.e., 1508-1512, state that the effect of legal prescription[62] becomes operative only when good faith has continued to exist, when the right or the object to be gained is prescriptible, and when there has lapsed the period of time postulated in the law. Such prescription is called acquisitive. Prescription is called extinctive when a person is freed from some obligation or duty, as detailed in canons 1701-1705.[63] The plaint of nullity against the sentence is proper to the Church's law and is regulated by that same law in the elements that relate to the legal prescription.[64]

The specific time limitation with regard to prospective judicial actions which encompass the irremediable nullity of a sentence is given as thirty years by the Code.[65] This period of thirty years is to be classed as a continuous duration of time which suffers no interruption,[66] and runs from the date of the publication of the sentence.[67] Therefore, the filing of suit for the plaint of nullity against an irremediably null sentence is outlawed after thirty years

[61] Cf. canon 1701. In the object which they prosecute, actions are either real or personal. Coronata, (*Institutiones Iuris Canonici*, III, n. 1193) states: Actio realis est qua iura nostra in re aut in rem independenter a persona qualibet iudicialiter nobis vindicamus. Actio personalis ea dicitur qua personam nobis obligatam ut aliquid nobis praestet prosequimur. Cf. also Lega, *Commentarius*, I, (1950) 361.

[62] Praescriptio est modus legitimus iuris acquirendi vel obligationis extinguendae procedens per possessionem modo et tempore a lege definito continuatam. — Lega, *op. cit.*, I, 478.

[63] Cf. Coronata, *Compendium Iuris Canonici* (2 vols., Taurini, 1938), n. 1681. In extinctive prescription a title is not required, and positive possession is not necessary; the possession of liberty is sufficient. — Coronata, *Institutiones Iuris Canonici*, III, n. 1231.

[64] Effectus est extinctivus actionis, inde habetur effectus rei acquisitivus in possessore. — Lega, *Commentarius*, I, (1950) 1024.

[65] Cf. canon 1893.

[66] Cf. canon 35; Roberti, *De Processibus*, II, n. 499; Goyeneche, *De Processibus*, I, 191-192.

[67] The years are to be reckoned according to the calendar, but the day of publication is not counted. — Cf. canon 34, § 3, 1°, 3°. Cf. also Roberti, *loc. cit.*; Goyeneche, *loc. cit.*

from the date on which the sentence was published.[68]

The plaint of nullity against a sentence of the Rota is to be proposed to the Apostolic Signatura.[69] The Apostolic Signatura decides the question whether or not the sentence of the Rota is null. After the Signatura has decided the question, the case is remanded to the Sacred Rota, unless the Supreme Pontiff provides otherwise.[70] If the plaint of nullity against a rotal sentence is joined cumulatively with an appeal, the subsequent operating panel of auditors (judges) decides the issue. The suit relating to the nullity of a sentence of the Apostolic Signatura is proposed before the Signatura itself.[71]

Section 2. Against Remediably Invalid Sentences

Canon 1895. *Querela nullitatis in casibus de quibus in can. 1894, proponi potest vel una cum appellatione intra decendium, vel seorsim et unice qua querela intra tres menses a die publicationis sententiae.*

The plaint of nullity against a sentence vitiated with remediable nullity can be lodged together with an appeal within ten days, or separately and by itself within three months from the day of the publication of the sentence.

The Code disallows an appeal from a sentence that is vitiated with nullity, for every appeal presupposes a valid sentence.[72] Canon 1895 declares, however, that the plaint of nullity can be proposed together with an appeal against a sentence vitiated with remediable nullity. In this regard, care must be taken that the plaint of nullity be combined with the allegation of injustice as an accessory motive, and not as the principal reason for the appeal; otherwise, the appeal will not be admitted.[73] When the plaint of nullity against a remediably null sentence is proposed together with an appeal, the norms that pertain to appeals are to be fol-

[68] Cf. canon 1893.
[69] Cf. canon 1603, § 1, 3°.
[70] Cf. canon 1604, § 3.
[71] Cf. Roberti, *De Processibus*, II, n. 496.
[72] Cf. canon 1880, 3°.
[73] Cf. Connolly, *Appeals*, p. 76; Roberti, *De Processibus*, II, n. 500.

lowed.[74] Consequently, this cumulative appeal, when lodged with the judge from whose sentence the appeal is taken, must be presented within ten days from the notice of the publication of the sentence.[75]

It should be noted that the time available for the introduction of the plaint of nullity against irremediably null sentences runs from the date of the publication of the sentence,[76] whereas the same remedy, joined with an appeal, against remediably null sentences runs from the notice of the publication of the sentence.[77]

The ten-day period set for the lodging of the cumulative appeal is absolutely of a peremptory nature, so that the failure to appeal within the ten days results in an abatement and anullment of that right.[78] The cumulative appeal may be made orally before the judge sitting in court if the sentence is read publicly, and it must then be immediately written down by the notary; otherwise the cumulative appeal is to be made in writing.[79] Since an appeal at the court of the appellate judge must be prosecuted within one month from the making of the appeal in the lower court, the same norm is to be followed in regard to the cumulative appeal, unless the judge against whose sentence the appeal is made grants more time for the prosecution of the appeal.[80] If the parties fail to act within the temporal limits set for the cumulative appeal, the appeal is considered relinquished.[81]

When the plaint of nullity against the sentence is joined with an appeal, the appellate court must give a decision on whether the sentence in the court of first instance is remediably null be-

[74] Cf. Roberti, *De Processibus*, II, n. 500.

[75] Cf. canon 1881. The reckoning of this period of ten days is regulated by canon 34, § 3, 3°. The first day is not counted. The ten-day period is considered as a *tempus utile*, i.e., the time for the exercise of one's right to appeal is granted in such a way that it does not run if one is prevented from using it through ignorance or through other inability to act at the time.—Cf. canon 35. Cf. also Connolly, *Appeals*, p. 104.

[76] Cf. canon 1893.

[77] Cf. canons 1881; 1895.

[78] Cf. canons 1634, § 1; 1881; Connolly, *Appeals*, pp. 103-104.

[79] Cf. canon 1882.

[80] Cf. canon 1883. Cf. also Connolly, *op. cit.*, pp. 160-161.

[81] Cf. canons 1634; 1886.

fore the appellate court proceeds with the principal issue.[82] If the plaint of nullity against a sentence is sustained, then all dependent related acts performed after the earlier rendered sentence are null and void. If the earlier sentence lacks motivation, the proper signatures, or the indications of time and place, the appellate court will remand the sentence to the court from which appeal is made. This allows for a correction and, at the instance of the interested party, for the repetition of the acts which followed after the publication of the sentence.[83] If, however, the judicial summons was missing, or if the summons was not legitimately served,[84] then the trial would have to be repeated at the instance of the interested party, because all the acts of the process would be null as well as the sentence.[85]

For the purpose of attacking the remediable nullity of a sentence, the plaint of nullity may also be proposed separately and by itself within three months from the date of the publication of the sentence.[86] When this remedy is proposed, the general norms which govern trials are to be adhered to, because no separate particular norms for procedure are set down in the Code.[87] The plaint of nullity against a remediably null sentence is proposed by means of a new judicial petition, which is to name the tribunal that is being called upon, to delineate the sentence that is being attacked, and to list the reasons on account of which the plaint of nullity is being proposed.[88] When the petition has been admitted by the judge, the other party, the promoter of justice, and the defender of the bond if he took part in the trial, are to be summoned. The joinder of issue then follows. The procedure continues in

[82] An appeal cannot be lodged against an invalid sentence. — Cf. canon 1880, 3°. Cf. also Roberti, *De Processibus*, II, n. 500; Connolly, *Appeals*, p. 76.

[83] Cf. canons 1680, §2; 1894; 1895. Cf. also Roberti, *loc. cit.*; "De sententia nullitatis vitio infecta," *Apollinaris*, IX (1936), 663, 664.

[84] Cf. *supra*, Chapter V, pp. 93-101.

[85] Cf. canons 1680, 1723; 1894, 1°. Cf. also Roberti, *De Processibus*, II, n. 489; Goyeneche, *De Processibus*, I, 189.

[86] Cf. canon 1895. In this event there will act as judge the one who issued the sentence. The question relating to the judges and the tribunal will be discussed as a separate Article of this Chapter, pp. 124-129.

[87] Cf. Roberti, *De Processibus*, II, n. 500; Goyeneche, *De Processibus*, I, 192.

[88] Cf. canon 1708; Roberti, *loc. cit.*; Goyeneche, *loc. cit.*

the ordinary manner and concludes with a sentence. The party has at his disposal all the remedies of law against the sentence.[89]

When a sentence has been declared remediably null because of a lack of the judicial summons or because the summons was not legitimately served on the defendant,[90] the process is also null and must be repeated at the instance of the interested party.[91] If the sentence lacks motivation, or the proper signatures, or the indications of time and place,[92] and the plaint of nullity against the sentence is sustained, these defects are subject to correction by the tribunal, and the act of publication of the sentence is to be repeated at the instance of the interested party.[93]

The specific time limitation with regard to the prospective use of the plaint of nullity against a remediably null sentence is indicated as three months from the date of the publication of the sentence.[94] This period of three months is considered as a continuous time which suffers no interruption,[95] and runs from the date of the publication of the sentence.[96] Therefore, the filing of suit for the plaint of nullity against a remediably null sentence is outlawed after three months from the date on which the sentence was published.[97]

If the plaint of nullity against the sentence has not been introduced nor the sentence amended within the time postulated in the law, the remediable nullity is considered sanated, provided that the sentence had been lawfully published.[98] This automatic

[89] Cf. Coronata, *Institutiones Iuris Canonici*, III, n. 1419; Wernz-Vidal, *Ius Canonicum*, VI, n. 620; Roberti, *loc. cit.*

[90] Cf. *supra*, Article 1 of Chapter V. pp. 93-101.

[91] Cf. canons 1723; 1894, 1o; Roberti, *De Processibus*, II, n. 489; Goyeneche, *De Processibus*, I, 189.

[92] Cf. *supra*, Articles 1 and 2 cf Chapter V.

[93] Cf. canons 1680, § 2; 1894, 2°, 3°; 1895. Cf. also Roberti, *loc. cit.*

[94] Cf. canon 1895.

[95] Cf. canon 35; Roberti, *op. cit.*, II, n. 499.

[96] The months are to be taken according to the calendar. The day of publication is not counted. — Cf. canon 34, § 3, 1°, 3°.

[97] Cf. canon 1895. Cf. *supra*, on prescription, Section 1 of this Article, pp. 118-119. No exception needs to be raised; it is simply the expiration of the time limit that brings about the automatic sanatation.

[98] Cf. Doheny, *Canonical Procedure*, I, 519; Roberti, *De Processibus*, II, n. 489.

sanation applies only to sentences vitiated with remediable nullity.[99] Moreover, if the parties know that the sentence is vitiated with remediable nullity and expressly or even tacitly condone this, it seems to be writer that the parties have given up their right to lodge the plaint of nullity. In such cases the sentence would be sanated.[100]

ARTICLE 3. THE JUDGE OF ORIGINAL JURISDICTION AND THE JUDGE OF APPEAL

Canon 1893. *Nullitas de qua in can. 1892 proponi potest . . . per modum vero actionis coram iudice qui sententiam tulit.*

The nullity of a sentence vitiated with the irremediable defects mentioned in canon 1892 can be attacked by means of an action before the judge who issued the sentence. By the term "judge," as used in this canon, is meant the ordinary tribunal of first and second instance, other than the Roman Rota, which issued the sentence.[101]

Canon 1895. *Querela nullitatis in casibus de quibus in can 1894, proponi potest . . . coram iudice qui sententiam tulit.*

The plaint of nullity against a sentence vitiated with remediable nullity in the causes considered in canon 1894 can be lodged before the judge who issued the sentence.

Before the time of the Code of Canon Law, it was admitted in practice to propose the action against the null sentence to the appellate judge. Scaccia declared that the action could be proposed before the judge who issued the sentence and also before the judge of the appellate court.[102] He maintained that if the plaint of nullity was proposed by itself, it could be lodged be-

[99] Cf. Roberti, *loc. cit.*; Vermeersch-Creusen, *Epitome*, III, n. 241; Coronata, *Institutiones Iuris Canonici*, III, n. 1418.

[100] Cf. Doheny, *Canonical Procedure*, I, 520.

[101] Cf. Roberti, *De Processibus*, II, n. 496.

[102] *Tractatus de Appellationibus*, Quaestio XIX, Rem. I, Concl. VI, nn. 1-2; Altimarus, *Tractatus de Nullitatibus in XIV Rubricas Divisus*, Rub. I, qu. 4, nn. 38-40.

fore the ordinary judge who pronounced the sentence or before the appellate judge. If the appellate tribunal was approached concerning the nullity of a sentence, this court could not only take cognizance of the nullity of the definitive sentence, but also could reform it or issue another sentence.[103]

This practice of proposing the plaint of nullity either before the judge who issued the sentence or before the appellate judge continued during the seventeenth and eighteenth centuries.[104] Bouix (1808-1870) stated that at his time the plaint of nullity was lodged only before the judge of appeal because of the current general custom.[105] Lega (1869-1935), however, maintained that the plaint of nullity was to be proposed before the same judge who issued the sentence. He stated in his pre-Code work, *Praelectiones de Iudiciis Civilibus* (1905), that according to the opinion of the doctors the plaint of nullity could be proposed likewise to the superior judge, but he refused to accept this procedure. Accordingly he held that, when there was question of the plaint of nullity which was in no way doubtful, then the judge who issued the sentence was to be approached, because less time was consumed and also the expense was less for the parties.[106]

The Code of Canon Law declares that, as an action, the plaint of nullity against the sentence vitiated with irremediable nullity is to be proposed before the judge who issued the sentence.[107] The plaint of nullity when invoked as an action against a sentence vitiated with remediable nullity is to be proposed before the judge who issued this sentence, if the plaint of nullity is lodged by itself and separately.[108] The judge who issued the sentence must not be understood to mean the same person who actually rendered the sentence. There is meant, rather, the same tribunal, for the individuals who constitute the present tribunal could be changed.[109]

It may be inferred from the Code that as a matter of rule the

[103] Scaccia, *op. cit.*, Quaestio XIX, Rem. I, Concl. VI, n. 73.

[104] Cf. *supra*, Section 2 of Article 2 in Chapter II, pp. 21-25.

[105] *Tractatus de Judiciis Ecclesiasticis*, II, 410.

[106] Lega, I, (1905) 690.

[107] Cf. canon 1893.

[108] Cf. canon 1895.

[109] Cf. Lega, *Commentarius*, II, 1030.

tribunal should not be changed for the obtaining of a decision regarding the plaint of nullity. The exception to this rule occurs when the plaint of nullity is joined with an appeal.[110]

If the party fears that the judge who pronounced the sentence which is attacked for either irremediable or remediable nullity may be prejudiced, and for that reason justly suspects him, he may demand that another judge, but in the same instance, be substituted for the hearing of the plaint of nullity against the sentence.[111] The party does not have to prove the reasonableness of his suspicion, since the mere fact that the judge pronounced the null sentence is sufficient reason to consider the judge suspect.[112]

When canons 1893 and 1895 state that the plaint of nullity is to be proposed "*coram iudice qui sententiam tulit*," do the canons mean only the ordinary judge and the judge who was delegated *ad universitatem causarum*, or also the judge who was delegated *ad causam*?

Noval maintains that a judge who was delegated for one cause cannot correct an invalid sentence once the sentence has been issued.[113] Wernz-Vidal exclude all delegated judges, even those who were delegated *ad universitatem causarum*, from having anything to do with their sentence.[114] There are other authors who follow this same view that the judge who was delegated for one cause cannot receive the plaint of nullity against the sentence.[115]

Vermeersch-Creusen[116] and other authors[117] maintain that a judge who was delegated for one cause can receive the plaint of nullity since the Code makes no distinction in these canons be-

[110] Cf. canon 1895; Roberti, *De Processibus*, II, n. 496.

[111] Cf. canons 1893; 1896; 1615.

[112] Cf. Noval, *De Iudiciis*, n. 663. Coronata believes that the judge should himself refrain from considering the plaint of nullity even though the exception of suspicion is not raised against him. — *Institutiones Iuris Canonici*, III, n. 1419.

[113] Cf. *De Iudiciis*, n. 660.

[114] Cf. *Ius Canonicum*, VI, n. 618.

[115] Cf. Bouix, II, 409; Lega, *Praelectiones de Iudiciis Civilibus* (1905), p. 689; *Commentarius*, II, 1030.

[116] Cf. *Epitome*, III, n. 242.

[117] Cf. Roberti, *De Processibus*, II, n. 497; Coronata, *Institutiones Iuris Canonici*, III, n. 1419.

tween ordinary and delegated judges. Another reason that is given is that the delegated judge has not completed his mandate by issuing a null sentence.[118]

The writer follows this latter opinion, for it seems reasonable to conclude that a delegated judge who has issued a null sentence has not fulfilled his mandate. Classical commentators, who maintained that the judge delegated *ad causam* had lost his authority and jurisdiction when he issued his sentence, believed, however, that there was an exception to this statement in the causes wherein the sentence was null because of failure to observe the formalities of his mandate.[119] Furthermore, to a person delegated with jurisdiction there is granted all power necessary to make his jurisdiction effective, even though a judge who is delegated *ad causam* must interpret his jurisdiction strictly.[120] When a delegated judge issues a sentence vitiated with nullity, what happens to the effectiveness of his jurisdiction if he should be forbidden to act on the plaint of nullity against his sentence? Moreover, canon 59, §1, states that an executor of a rescript who has in any way erred in executing the same, may again resume the execution of the same rescript. From at least the analogy in regard to the execution of rescripts, the writer believes that in matters of judicial jurisdiction there is no reason why the judge who is delegated *ad causam* cannot resume the process in order to bring it to a valid end.[121]

Canons 1893 and 1895 make no distinction when they decree that the plaint of nullity may be proposed before the judge who issued the sentence. Consequently, the writer maintains that the delegated judge should not be excluded. In addition, canon 1897, §2, does not exclude the judge delegated *ad causam* from reviewing or amending a sentence issued by him.[122]

[118] Cf. canons 59, § 1; 1606; 207, § 1.

[119] Cf. Reiffenstuel, lib. II, tit. 28, n. 30; Pichler, lib. II, tit. 28, n. 5; Engel, lib. II, tit. 28, n. 4.

[120] Cf. canon 200, § 1.

[121] Cf. Roberti, *De Processibus*, II, n. 497, note 2; Vermeersch-Creusen, *Epitome*, III, n. 242.

[122] The judge *ex officio* can review and amend the null sentence if he can accomplish this without a new process. — Cf. Goyeneche, *De Processibus*, I, 191; Roberti, *De Processibus*, II, n. 497.

If the plaint of nullity is proposed immediately after the publication of the sentence which is vitiated with such remediable nullities which affect only the sentence,[123] it seems reasonable that the judge who has issued the sentence should be in a position to correct his errors. If the plaint of nullity is proposed after a longer period of time, or if the sentence is vitiated with a defect which upsets the whole process, it seems better — even though the judge delegated *ad causam* has authority to receive the plaint— to propose the plaint of nullity before the ordinary, so that he may decide whether to commit the cause to the first delegated judge or to other judges whether ordinary or delegated.[124]

The plaint of nullity against a sentence vitiated with remediable nullity can also be proposed along with an appeal within ten days from the notice of the publication of the sentence. In such an event, the appellate tribunal is approached; and the norms that pertain to appeals are followed.[125] When the plaint of nullity against a sentence is joined with an appeal, the plaint of nullity is combined with the appeal as an accessory motive, and not as the principal reason for the appeal.[126]

A question that arises concerning the plaint of nullity is whether or not this remedy could be joined with an appeal for an attack upon an irremediably null sentence. Authors do not generally discuss the question. Lega believes that one could join the plaint of nullity with an appeal in order to attack not only a sentence vitiated with remediable nullity but also a sentence null in consequence of irremediable nullity.[127] The writer does not agree with Lega in this opinion, for canon 1893, which refers specifically to the irremediable nullities listed in canon 1892, does not mention the plaint of nullity as a remedy that may be joined with an appeal; it mentions the plaint of nullity as employable in the nature of an exception and also in the nature of an action before

[123] Cf. canon 1894, 2°, 3°, 4°.

[124] Cf. Roberti, *loc. cit.*; Goyeneche, *De Processibus*, I, 191.

[125] Cf. Roberti, *De Processibus*, II, n. 500.

[126] Cf. Roberti, *loc. cit.* Cf. also *supra*, Article 2 of this Chapter under Section 2 for a detailed treatment of the cumulative appeal.

[127] Cf. *Commentarius*, II, 1029.

the judge who issued the sentence. Canon 1895 alone speaks of this joint remedy, and it considers the cumulative appeal only in regard to remediable nullity.[128]

If the plaint of remediable nullity against the sentence is not proposed immediately after the publication of the sentence, the judge may *ex officio* cancel an invalid sentence issued by him, and amend it within the limits stated by the law.[129] In criminal trials, and in matters concerning the public weal of the Church or the salvation of souls, the judge is obliged to take action *ex officio*.[130] The judge may also take cognizance of the remediable nullity of his sentence which involves private interests only, for the sentence of a trial concerns the public good since it is essential to the proper administration of justice. The judge should do this all the more when the nullity affects only the sentence and not the process. The judge, however, cannot, independently of the will of the parties, re-institute the process in causes that simply concern the private good.[131]

Article 4. Parties Involved

Canon 1897, §1. *Querelam nullitatis interponere possunt nedum partes, quae se gravatas putant, sed etiam promotor iustitiae aut defensor vinculi, quoties iudicio interfuerunt.*

The plaint of nullity against the sentence may be introduced not only by the parties who think themselves aggrieved, but also by the promoter of justice or by the defender of the bond, whenever either has taken part in the trial.

[128] Cf. Coronata, *Institutiones Iuris Canonici*, III, n. 1419; Roberti, *De Processibus*, II, n. 496; Noval, *De Iudiciis*, nn. 660, 662.

[129] Cf. canon 1897, § 2; 1894, 2°, 3°, 4°.

[130] Cf. canon 1618.

[131] Cf. Roberti, *De Processibus*, II, n. 498; Coronata, *Institutiones Iuris Canonici*, III, n. 1420; Goyeneche, *De Processibus*, I, 191. Lega, on the contrary, stated that canon 1897, § 2, does not apply in purely contentious causes in which only private interests are involved. — *Commentarius*, II, 1032. The writer believes that this opinion of Lega fails to take into account that the nullity of a sentence does concern the public good.

The parties to the trial can propose the plaint of nullity against an irremediably invalid sentence: 1) if it has been issued by an absolutely incompetent tribunal or in a collegiate tribunal by a number of judges that fails to respond to the demand made in canon 1576, §1;[132] 2) if the sentence has been issued to parties of whom at least one did not have any rightful standing in the court,[133] and 3) if somebody acted in the name of another without a legitimate mandate.[134] Inasmuch as these irremediable nullities have been established for the public good, the parties in a trial cannot renounce them.[135] In other words, the parties can never sanate a sentence vitiated with any of these irremediable nullities.[136]

The parties may attack the sentence which is null in consequence of the nullities mentioned in canon 1892 through their proposal of the plaint of nullity as an action before the judge who issued the sentence. The parties can do this within thirty years from the date of publication of the sentence, or they may propose the plaint of nullity as an exception at any future time.[137]

The parties in a trial may also propose the plaint of nullity against the sentence when it is vitiated with a remediable nullity, i.e., 1) if there was no legitimate summons;[138] 2) if the sentence does not contain mention of the motives or the reasons for the decision, with the exception of the sentences of the Apostolic Signatura;[139] 3) if the sentence is not subscribed by the persons who must sign it, and 4) and if it does not bear a notation of the year, the month, and the day on which and the place in which the sentence was pronounced.[140] Inasmuch as these remediable nullities rest upon reasons which directly concern the private ad-

[132] Cf. canons 1892, 1°; 1897, § 1. Cf. also *supra*, Articles 1 and 2 of Chapter IV.

[133] Cf. canons 1892, 2°; 1897, § 1. Cf. also *supra*, Article 3 of Chapter IV.

[134] Cf. canon 1892, 3°. Cf. also *supra*, Article 4 of Chapter IV.

[135] Cf. Lega, *Commentarius*, II, 1015; Vermeersch-Creusen, *Epitome*, III, n. 241.

[136] Cf. Doheny, *Canonical Procedure*, I, 514.

[137] Cf. canon 1893. Cf. also *supra*, Articles 1 and 2 of Chapter VI.

[138] Cf. canons 1894, 1°; 1897, § 1. Cf. also *supra*, Article I of Chapter V.

[139] Cf. canon 1894, 2°. Cf. also *supra*, Article 2 of Chapter V.

[140] Cf. canon 1894, 3°, 4°. Cf. also *supra*, Article 3 of Chapter V.

vantage of the parties, the parties in a trial may renounce or waive these nullities, either expressly or tacitly, by not using the remedy within the postulated time limit.[141]

The parties have at their disposal the plaint of nullity to attack a sentence vitiated with these remediable nullities. They may propose the plaint of nullity together with the appeal within ten days from the notification of the publication of the sentence, or they may lodge the plaint of nullity separately and by itself as an action within three months from the date of the publication of the sentence. In this latter event the remedy is to be lodged before the judge who issued the sentence.[142]

If a party fears that the judge who pronounced the sentence which is attacked for nullity may be prejudiced, or for that reason justly suspects him, he may demand that another judge, but in the same court, be substituted for the first judge.[143] If the parties realize that the sentence is remediably null and expressly or even tacitly condone this, it seems that they forfeit their right to introduce the plaint of nullity. However, if the parties do not realize that the sentence is remediably null and no one informs them of this and no further action is taken by anyone, the remediable nullity will be automatically sanated upon the expiration of the time stipulated in law.[144]

Even the victorious party has the right to propose the plaint of nullity against the sentence inasmuch as through its extension he may suffer harm, since upon the introduction of this plaint such a sentence cannot be lawfully executed.[145]

[141] Cf. Lega, *Commentarius*, II, 1015; Wernz-Vidal, *Ius Canonicum*, VI, n. 614.

[142] Cf. canons 1895; 1881.

[143] Cf. canon 1615; 1896. The fact that the judge pronounced the null sentence is sufficient reason to consider him suspect. — Cf. Noval, *De Iudiciis*, n. 663; Coronata, *Institutiones Iuris Canonici*, III, n. 1419.

[144] Cf. Doheny, *Canonical Procedure*, I, 520; canon 1895. The parties can employ the plea for a *restitutio in integrum* if through lapse of time they have forfeited the plaint of nullity, but they must do this in accordance with canon 1687.

[145] Cf. Coronata, *Institutiones Iuris Canonici*, III, n. 1420; Roberti, *De Processibus*, II, n. 498.

Since the parties in a trial have the right to propose the plaint of nullity against the sentence, they can do this either personally or through their procurator.[146] The same rights avail for the heirs or the successors of either party to the suit.[147] The exercise of this right comes into play when one of the litigants dies, when he changes his state of life, or when he gives up the office in connection with which he became involved in litigation.

Moreover, guardians and tutors, when designated for a specific trial (*ad litem*), can also propose the plaint against the sentence when their ward is a principal in the trial.[148] In addition to the parties, the promoter of justice and also the defender of the bond, when they have taken part in the trial, may also propose the plaint of nullity against the sentence.[149]

The defender of the bond takes part in causes wherein there is question of the validity of sacred orders or of marriages.[150] It is the duty of the defender of the bond to uphold the validity of the marriage and of sacred orders, and to take part in these trials. He accordingly may institute the plaint of nullity against the sentence vitiated with the irremediable nullities specified in canon 1892, when that sentence sustains the invalidity of the sacred orders or the marriage.[151] He may also propose the plaint of nullity against a sentence sustaining their invalidity when it is null in consequence of the remediable nullities specified in canon 1894. This the defender of the bond could easily accomplish by joining the plaint of nullity with his appeal within the ten-day period,[152] or he could likewise propose the plaint of nullity before the court which rendered the sentence. This proposal he would have to make within three months from the date of publication of the

[146] Cf. Lega, *Commentarius*, II, 1031. Special authorization of the procurator is unnecessary provided that the original judicial mandate has not been revoked. — Cf. Hogan, *Judicial Advocates and Procurators*, p. 115. Cf. also *supra*, Article 4 of Chapter IV.

[147] Cf. canon 1733, 2°.

[148] Cf. Lega, *loc. cit.* Cf. also *supra*, Article 3 of Chapter IV.

[149] Cf. canon 1897, § 1.

[150] Cf. canon 1586.

[151] Cf. canon 1897, § 1; Wernz-Vidal, *Ius Canonicum*, VI, n. 617.

[152] Cf. canon 1895.

sentence.[153] The Code demands that within ten days the defender of the bond make an appeal from a sentence which declares the nullity of a marriage; if he neglects his duty, he shall be forced to do so by the authority of the judge.[154] If the null sentence is vitiated with remediable nullity, can the defender of the bond refuse to join the plaint of nullity with his appeal? The Code does not state this as an obligation for the defender of the bond as it does in regard to his making the appeal.[155] The Code, however, does state that there can not be a simple appeal from a sentence that is null and void.[156] An appeal always presupposes a valid sentence. Therefore, the writer believes that in such causes the defender of the bond must combine the plaint of nullity as an accessory motive with the appeal.[157] Consequently the defender of the bond is not practically concerned with the three-month period fixed for the separate invoking of the plaint of nullity, and least of all when he seeks a redress against the sentence of nullity, pronounced by the court of first instance.[158]

The promoter of justice is to appear and take part in all criminal causes, and also in such contentious causes in which the ordinary believes the public welfare is in issue.[159] The presence of the promoter of justice is necessary in all criminal causes because the introducing of a criminal action or suit is reserved exclusively to him.[160] The promoter of justice is also to take part in contentious causes which involve the public good, and in many other causes in which the public good may probably become involved.[161]

[153] Cf. canon 1895.

[154] Cf. canons 1881, 1986.

[155] Cf. canon 1986.

[156] Cf. canon 1880, 3°.

[157] Cf. Roberti, *De Processibus*, II, n. 500; Connolly, *Appeals*, p. 76.

[158] Cf. Dolan, *The Defensor Vinculi*, The Catholic University of America Canon Law Studies, n. 85 (Washington, D.C.: The Catholic University of America, 1934), p. 121.

[159] Cf. canon 1586.

[160] Cf. canon 1934.

[161] Cf. canon 1586. Public good is synonymous with the general welfare and the salvation of the faithful. It includes not only a defense of the public ecclesiastical order, but also the intervention in private affairs as often as these affairs may affect the common welfare. — Cf. Glynn, *The Promoter of*

For example, the public good may demand that certain marriages or ordinations which cannot be impugned by anyone else than the promoter of justice be declared null. There may be question of the defense of minors or of juridical persons. The public good is also involved in the regulation of certain procedural questions such as the declaration of nullity of a sentence previously pronounced by the court. The ordinary will also judge when the public good in involved in private affairs, or when the public good is in danger of being compromised.[162]

The promoter of justice has the right to propose the plaint of nullity against the sentence.[163] "It makes no difference whether the sentence was favorable or unfavorable to him and in criminal trials whether it was condemnatory or absolving in character, for it pertains to the public good that sentences involving that good which are certainly null be set aside and the error repaired by a repetition of the process."[164] If the process must be repeated, the promoter of justice will take steps to have this done only when the public good demands this procedure, and when it is evident from the trial that the cause pertains to the public good and that a reversal can result in a decision favorable to the common welfare of the diocese.[165]

The promoter of justice may propose the plaint of nullity against a sentence vitiated with irremediable nullity either as an exception or as an action before the tribunal which rendered it. The filing of the suit must ensue within thirty years from the date of the publication of the sentence.[166] If the sentence is vitiated with remediable nullity, the promoter of justice, if he takes part in the cause, may propose the plaint of nullity together with his appeal within the ten-day period, or as a separate action within

Justice, The Catholic University of America Canon Law Studies, n. 101 (Washington, D.C.: The Catholic Univesity of America, 1936), p. 86; Noval, *De Iudiciis*, n. 123.

162 Cf. Glynn, *op. cit.*, pp. 88-89; 92; Roberti, *De Processibus*, II, n. 122.

163 Cf. canon 1897, § 1.

164 Cf. Glynn, *The Promoter of Justice*, p. 312; Noval, *De Iudiciis*, n. 502.

165 Cf. Glynn, *op. cit.*, p. 314.

166 Cf. canon 1893.

three months, before the tribunal which rendered the sentence.[167]

When the parties in a trial propose the plaint of nullity against the sentence, the promoter of justice should also be present to assist in the matter, for the nullity of a judicial sentence always affects the public good.[168] If the promoter of justice or the defender of the bond must take part in a trial, but were not present,[169] the acts are invalid. The plaint of nullity, however, is not the remedy with which to attack the sentence which concluded such a trial. The reason for this statement is that canons 1892 and 1894 do not list this defect among the causes of irremediable or remediable nullity.[170]

The writer finds himself in complete agreement with the statement of Glynn who declared that in all the causes that concern the nullity of a sentence "the promoter of justice will endeavor to protect all that has accrued to the public good in virtue of the sentence which is now attacked on technical grounds and in the event that it is decided that the sentence is null, he will take proper steps to retrieve for the public good whatever has been lost to it by the declaration that the sentence of the first instance was null."[171]

[167] Cf. canon 1895.

[168] Cf. Wernz,Vidal, *Ius Canonicum*, VI, 620; Roberti, *De Processibus*, II, n. 498.

[169] Cf. canon 1587, § 1.

[170] Whether the listings of canons 1892 and 1894 are merely demonstrative or all-inclusive, will be discussed in the following Chapter.

[171] Cf. Glynn, *The Promoter of Justice*, p. 315.

CHAPTER VII

INTERPRETATION OF CANONS 1892 AND 1894

The Code of Canon Law in canons 1892 and 1894 determines the causes which support the plaint of nullity against the sentence. Are the enumerations of causes as given in these two canons to be considered fully exclusive?[1] Or, are defects in the application of purely procedural law when they cause the nullity of certain acts of the trial to be included, so that the plaint of nullity can be proposed also against such sentences?

The question of the interpretation of canons 1892 and 1894 is closely connected with the proper understanding and interpretation of the phrase "*praescriptum legis evidenter neglectum*" in canon 1905, §2, 4° — i.e., whether the plea for a *restitutio in integrum* can be lodged against a sentence which concludes a process that reflects the neglect of some provision specified in the procedural law. There is no agreement among the authors on this question. Roberti[2] and some other authors[3] maintain that this enumeration is not exclusive, so that sentences which are null because of some other procedural defects may be challenged with the plaint of nullity against the sentence. In other words, these authors exclude from canon 1905, §2, 4°, the violation of a purely formal procedural law.

In opposition to this extensive interpretation, which will be referred to as the opinion of Roberti, there is the opinion of D'Angelo (1885-1930)[4] and of those who sustain a exclusive inter-

[1] "Dicimus exclusivam, non taxativam, quia vix fieri potest ut nullitates iure positivo statutae non sint taxative; in hoc enim casu evanesceret finis ipsius enumerationis." — Cf. Roberti, *De Processibus*, II, n. 492.

[2] *De Processibus*, II, nn. 520-523; "Circa limites querelae nullitatis et restitutionis in integrum," *Apollinaris*, I (1928), 476-483.

[3] Hanssen, "De sanctione nullitatis in processu canonicao," *Apollinaris*, XII (1939), 238-249; Lemieux, *The Sentence in Eclesiastical Procedure*, pp. 99, 102; Hogan, *Judicial Advocates and Procurators*, p. 169.

[4] "De Restitutione in Integrum," *Periodica de Religiosis et Missionariis*

pretation with reference to the defects enumerated in canons 1892 and 1894.[5] D'Angelo believed that the plea for a *restitutio in integrum* is the proper remedy against a sentence vitiated with other defects than those listed in canons 1892 and 1894, provided that the damage sustained through the sentence is grave. In other words, these latter authors maintain that the plaint of nullity can be proposed only against a sentence that it vitiated with the nullities expressly mentioned in canons 1892 and 1894.

Still another opinion on this subject is advanced by Crnica. He declares that an extensive interpretation cannot be applied either to the canons on the plaint of nullity against the sentence or to the phrase *legis praescriptum.* He concludes, therefore, that the Code does not provide any specific remedy against a sentence which is null in consequence of a defect of procedural law if such defect is not mentioned in canons 1892 and 1894.[6] Such an opinion, in the mind of the present writer, is of no practical help, for it seems actually to evade the issue.[7]

It must be noted, however, that the interpretation which is given to the canons that deal with the plaint of nullity and the interpretation which is accorded to canon 1905, §2, 4°, are not necessarily interdependent.[8]

(Brugis, 1905-1919); *Periodica de Re Canonica et Morali, utilia Praesertim Religiosis et Missionariis* (Brugis, 1920-1927); *Periodica de Re Morali, Canonica, Liturgica* (Brugis, 1927-1936; Romae, 1937-), XVIII (1929), 37* - 62* (hereafter this will be referred to as *Periodica*).

[5] Coronata, *Institutiones Iuris Canonici,* III, n. 1418; Wernz-Vidal, *Ius Canonicum,* VI, n. 623; Muniz, *Procedimientos Ecclesiasticos* (2. ed., 3 vols., Seville: Lib. de Sobrino de Izquierdo, 1926), III, n. 505; Feeney, *Restitutio in Integrum,* pp. 111-130; Blat, *De Processibus,* n. 438; Vermeersch-Creusen, *Epitome,* III, n. 246. Lega maintained that the causes of remediable nullity as mentioned in canon 1894 are not all-inclusive, but he did include formal precedural laws under the term *legis praescriptum.* — *Commentarius,* II, 1025-1026.

[6] Cf. "Defectus Codicis I.C. in designandis normis pro querela nullitatis,"— *Jus Pontificium,* XV (1935), 145-155.

[7] Feeney states that this opinion of Crnica simply begs the question and is of no aid in interpreting the law at present. — *Restitutio in Integrum,* p. 113.

[8] Feeney, *Restitutio in Integrum,* p. 113; Noone, *Nullity in Judicial Acts,* p. 107.

Reference will be made to the plea for a *restitutio in integrum* only in so far as this remedy pertains to the discussion on the plaint of nullity against the sentence, for the writer is concerned primarily with the plaint of nullity against the sentence, and not with the plea for a *restitutio in integrum.*

Article 1. The Extensive Interpretation

Roberti's opinion states that the list of defects enumerated in canons 1892 and 1894 is not all-inclusive. The proponents of this opinion believe that a sentence may be null for other reasons and can, therefore, be attacked with the plaint of nullity against the sentence.[9]

The Code decrees that the nullity of every act is governed either by positive law or by the natural law,[10] that is, if some essential constituents of the act are wanting or if there are lacking some formalities or conditions which the canons require under pain of nullity. The nullity of an act can be either original or derived.[11] Nullity is original if the act labors under its own defect, whereas it is derived if the act is null because of the nullity of some other act in the process upon which it depends.[12] The sentence of a trial is vitiated with original nullity when the defect originates in the sentence itself; and with derived nullity, when the sentence, which of itself is perfect, is the result of an invalid process, or when it is based on invalid acts within the process.[13] In the procedural law of the Code[14] there are certain formalities whose omission causes the nullity of the acts of the trial. For example, the acts which are not drawn up by the notary or not subscribed by

[9] Cf. Roberti, *De Processibus,* II, n. 491.

[10] Cf. canon 1680, § 1.

[11] Cf. canon 1680, § 2.

[12] Cf. Roberti, *De Processibus,* I (1. ed.), n. 241.

[13] Cf. Roberti, *De Processibus,* II, n. 487.

[14] Substantive law deals with the rights of persons, whereas procedural law is concerned with the rules of the judicial process — the constitution of tribunals, the form of judicial acts, etc. Procedural law is the form related to substantive law, although some procedural laws are substantive when they grant some good, e.g., norms which grant actions. — Cf. Roberti, *op. cit.,* I, n. 18.

him are null;[15] in causes which require the presence of the promoter of justice or the defender of the bond, the acts are null and void if in the absence of a summons they were not present;[16] prejudicial attempts against a party to a lawsuit are automatically null and void;[17] and the renunciation of a judicial instance or of the acts of the cause is null if it is not done as prescribed in the law.[18] The sentence which concludes an invalid process is null because of derived nullity in consequence of the ruling enunciated in canon 1680, §2. Any defect, according to Roberti, which violates the natural law or the positive law would consequently cause the nullity of a sentence. Roberti's interpretation of certain decisions of the Rota and the Signatura is supposed to bear out this contention.[19]

The plaint of nullity can be proposed against any sentence null in consequence of derived nullity, even though the cause of such nullity is not stated in canons 1892 and 1894. There are other demonstrative listings in the Code of Canon Law which give the appearance of being restrictive listings.[20] Consequently, the defects enumerated in canons 1892 and 1894 constitute only a demonstrative listing, even as canon 1902 does, though it seems to provide an all-inclusive listing.[21]

The phrase, "*legis praescriptum evidenter neglectum*," of canon 1905, §2, 4°, cannot be interpreted to include violations of formal procedural law.[22] Although canon 1905, §2, 4°, speaks absolute-

[15] Cf. canon 1585, § 1.

[16] Cf. canon 1587, § 1.

[17] Cf. canon 1855, § 1.

[18] Cf. canon 1740, § 2.

[19] Cf. S.R.R., *Mauranen. seu Camberien*, 13 jul. 1918 — *AAS*, XI (1919), 395; Signatura, *Paderbornen.*, 10 mart. 1919 — *AAS*, XI (1919), 296-297; *De Manila*, 6 apr. 1920 — *AAS*, XII (1920), 256. Cf. also Roberti, *De Processibus*, II, nn. 493, 494.

[20] Cf. canon 1902. This canon lists causes which are considered as *res iudicata*, yet a cause which has been appealed can become irrevocably adjudged when there has intervened an abatement or a renunciation, which fact is not mentioned in canon 1902. — Cf. Roberti, "Circa limites querelae nullitatis et restitutionis in integrum," *Apollinaris*, I (1928), 477.

[21] Cf. Roberti, *De Processibus*, II, n. 492.

[22] The neglect of a law can be either positive, an action contrary to the

ly, the term *lex* is concerned with substantive law in paragraph two, number four and not with formal procedural law. The plea for a *restitutio in integrum* avails for an attack on an unjust sentence, which results from the violation of substantive law, and not an illegitimate sentence which results from the violation of formal procedural law.[23] The plea for a *restitutio in integrum* has as a fixed purpose the repairing of injustice; but if a sentence labors only under a defect of form, there is no reason for granting the plea for a *restitutio in integrum*, because the new sentence would merely confirm the old sentence. In addition, many abuses will arise if one can invoke the remedy of the plea for a *restitutio in integrum* with reference to the violation of procedural law. Even if this remedy were granted only for the more grave violations, too much latitude would be given to the judge in deciding what violations caused grave damage.[24]

In 1834 Pope Gregory XVI (1831-1846) in his *Regolamento legislativo e guidiciario*[25] confirmed the use of the plea for a *restitutio in integrum* when there was neglect of some law or an express contravention of some law in force.[26] The *Regulae Servandae* of the Signatura in 1912 changed the law of Gregory XVI, so that the neglect of a law or an express violation of some law in force was to serve as a motive for the plaint of nullity.[27]

If canon 1905, §2, 4°, is similar to the law of Gregory XVI, the similarity exists only as to the inclusion of substantive law,

law, or negative, an omission of consideration of some law. — Cf. Feeney, *Restitutio in Integrum*, p. 111.

[23] Cf. Roberti, *De Processibus*, II, n. 522; Hanssen, "art. cit.," *Apollinaris*, XII (1939), 242.

[24] Cf. Roberti, *loc. cit.*

[25] Cf. *Acta Gregorii Papae XVI*, IV, 300-410. Cf. also *supra*, Chapter II, p. 30.

[26] Cf. *Regolamento*, §1058 — *Acta Gregorii Papae XVI*, IV, 365. Feeney states that a distinction was made between the *restitutio* for the neglect of substantive law and *restitutio* for the *neglect of formal procedural law*. — *Restitutio in Integrum*, p. 117. It must be conceded, nevertheless, that regardless of this distinction the *restitutio* was granted.

[27] Cf. *Regulae servandae in iudiciis apud Supremum Signaturae Ap. Tribunal*, 6 mart. 1912, art. 4 — *AAS*, IV (1912), 189; *Fontes*, n. 6462.

and not of procedural law, under the *restitutio in integrum*.[28] Roberti states that the Code of Canon Law has reserved the violations of the formal procedural law to the plaint of nullity, and that the violations of the substantive law, which render the sentence unjust rather than null, were disjoined from the plaint of nullity and placed among the factors with reference to which the plea for a *restitutio in integrum* could serve as the proper remedy at law.[29] As a result, the proponents of this opinion hold that canons 1892 and 1894 are to be interpreted extensively, so as to include also the various violations of procedural law. Such sentences then are to be attacked with the plaint of nullity.[30]

The writer does not agree with Roberti and Hansen in their contention that canons 1892 and 1894 do not contain an all-inclusive listing. The arguments advanced for their opinion certainly seem not conclusive.

It is the opinion of the writer that canon 1680 in regard to judicial sentences must be interpreted in the light of the canons on the plaint of nullity. The general law of canon 1680 is definitely limited by the canons on the plaint of nullity.[31] If canon 1680 serves as the basis for an action of nullity against a sentence vitiated with defects other than those stated in canons 1892 and 1894, certainly this action is not the *querela nullitatis contra sententiam*.

Furthermore, canon 1902 does not furnish a merely demonstrative listing of what constitutes the *res iudicata*, though, according to Roberti, this canon seems to point to a restrictive listing. Roberti's statement that an abatement of the trial and the renunciation of an appeal are not included among the factors that engender a *res iudicata* is not correct, since either the abatement of a trial or also the renunciation of an appeal can under canon 1902

[28] Cf. Feeney, *Restitutio in Integrum*, p. 117.

[29] Cf. Roberti, *De Processibus*, II, nn. 486, 522.

[30] Cf. Roberti, *op. cit.*, I, nn. 228-231.

[31] Cf. Noone, *Nullity in Judicial Acts*, p. 119; Feeney, *Restitutio in Integrum*, p. 121.

[32] Cf. Roberti, "Circa limites querelae nullitatis et restitutionis in integrum," *Apollinaris*, I (1928), 477. Cf. also canon 1736; 1740.

be regarded as a deserted appeal.[32]

Roberti declares that the violation of the formal procedural law results in an illegitimate sentence, and not in an unjust sentence. Consequently, so he argues, the plea for a *restitutio in integrum* cannot be employed for the purpose of attacking illegitimate sentences.[33] Such an opinion seems not admissible, for a sentence can be rendered unjust through the violation of formal procedural law. The violation of procedural law is a violation of the party's right to have his cause tried according to the due process of law. Moreover, the Church has imposed procedural formalities to ensure justice; when they are neglected, the judge acts unjustly.[34]

The argument of Roberti that, if the *restitutio* were granted for the violation of formal procedural law, then too much latitude would thereby be given to the judge in deciding what violations cause grave damage,[35] is itself open to a new problem. The problem namely is this: It will not at all be beyond dispute which of the violations of procedural law unmentioned in canons 1892 and 1894 will vitiate a sentence only with remediable rather than irremediable nullity.[36]

In regard to the jurisprudence of the Roman tribunals as cited by the defenders of the extensive interpretation, the decisions for the most part are all pre-Code decisions.[37] These decisions certainly cannot be a guide to the proper interpretation of canon 1905, §2, 4°, because the Rota and the authors themselves admit that the law has changed.[38] Several decisions since the enactment of the Code may seem to approve the extensive interpretation of

[33] Cf. Roberti, *De Processibus*, II, n. 522; Hanssen, "art cit.," *Apollinaris*, XII (1939), 242.

[34] Cf. Feeney, *Restitutio in Integrum*, p. 122.

[35] Cf. Roberti, *De Processibus*, II, n. 522.

[36] Cf. Feeney, *op. cit.*, p. 123; Noone, *Nullity in Judicial Acts*, p. 120.

[37] Cf. Roberti, *De Processibus*, II, nn. 493, 494; Hanssen, "art. cit.," *Apollinaris*, XII (1939), 246.

[38] Cf. Roberti, *op. cit.*, II, nn. 514, 516; Hanssen, *loc. cit.* Cf. also *S. Iacobi de Chile*, 5 iul. 1927: coram R.P.D. Parrillo, dec. XXXIV, n. 4 — *Decisiones*, XIX (1927), 278.

canons 1892 and 1894. The decisions, however, of the Signatura[39] cannot serve as a guide to the lower tribunals, for the Signatura acts according to its own *Regulae* as interpreted by the Chirograph of Benedict XV.[40] The Rota decisions which seem to be in favor of Roberti's opinion really are inconclusive. One decision[41] was apparently decided on the old law, since the nullities of the old law were the only ones mentioned. A decree of the Rota is quoted by Roberti in support of his opinion, but the decree does not support Roberti's opinion according to the view of the writer.[42] Another decision given by the Rota in 1930 states that a sentence would be null in view of a defect not mentioned in canon 1892.[43] In another suit, however, but for the same reason, the Rota granted the plea for a *restitutio in integrum* in virtue of canon 1905, §2, 4°.[44]

Article 2. The Exclusive Interpretation

D'Angelo's opinion maintains that the list of defects as stated in canons 1892 and 1894 is all-inclusive. This opinion holds that, when a sentence is null for reasons other than those stated in canons 1892 and 1894, the remedy to be employed is the appeal or the plea for a *restitutio in integrum*, and not the plaint of nullity.[45]

Various arguments are advanced in support of this exclusive

[39] Cf. *Paderbornen*, 31 maii 1919 — *AAS*, XI (1919), 297; *De Manila*, 6 apr. 1920 — *AAS*, XII (1920), 256.

[40] Cf. Benedictus XV, chirograph. *Attentis expositis*, 28 iun. 1915 (*Appendix ad regulas servandas in iudiciis apud Supremum Signaturae Ap. Tribunal*, art. 1) — *AAS*, VII (1915), 320-325; *Fontes*, after n. 6462.

[41] Cf. *Mauranen. seu Camberien.*, 13 iul. 1918 — *AAS*, XI (1919), 392-404.

[42] In the decree *Decretum*, 28 iul. 1931, canon 1892, 2° — lack of procedural capacity — was cited as the cause of nullity, and not the absence of the promoter of justice — *AAS*, XXIV (1932), 99.

[43] The illegitimate denial of the right to defend oneself against a declaration of contumacy was the defect. — Cf. *Proprietatis*, 27 febr. 1930, dec. XI, n. 4 — *Decisiones*, XXII (1930), 120.

[44] Cf. *Incidentis super contumacia*, 24 iul. 1923, dec. XXI — *Decisiones*, XV (1923), 180-189.

[45] D'Angelo, "De Restitutione in integrum," *Periodica*, XVIII (1929), p. 38.*

interpretation. A comparison of canons 1892 and 1894 with the *Schemata* drawn up prior to the Code clearly shows that the *Schemata* included the plaint of nullity as a remedy for any defect of nullity, notably the case in which the process itself labored under some defect of nullity.[46] Canons 1892 and 1894, however, do not mention the nullity of the process as a defect vitiating the sentence. Moreover, canon 403, n. 2, of the same *Schema*[47] makes mention of an evident error of fact, e.g., a sentence based on false documents. Although this was listed under the plaint of nullity in the *Schema*, it now appears in the Code as a basis of the plea for a *restitutio in integrum*.[48]

D'Angelo rejected the argument concerning canon 1680 as referring to the sentence, and maintained that the nullity of the act as mentioned in this canon really refers to an act in the sense of *negotium*.[49]

Another argument advanced in support of the exclusive interpretation is obtained from an examination of the sources of law as found in the footnotes added to the Code.[50] The footnotes list-

[46] *Schema*, F. can. 403 states: "Sententia vitio nullitatis laborat quando: . . . n. 5: Ipse processus vitio nullitatis est infectus, e.g. . . ." — *Codicis Iuris Canonici Schemata, Lib. I V, De Processibus, I, De Iudiciis in Genere*, p. 437. Every indication is that this canon 403, n. 5, gives a demonstrative list of nullities, and not an all-inclusive one. Cf. also *Schema* B, can. 295, n. 6, p. 436; *Schema* D, can. 428, n. 5, p. 436; *Schema E*, can. 449, n. 5, p. 437.

[47] Cf. *Schema* F, can. 403, n. 2, p. 435.

[48] "De restitutione in Integrum," *Periodia*, XVIII (1929)m pp. 42*, 45.*

[49] D'Angelo maintained that canon 1680 "agitur de actu (negotio) iuridico, de materia, nempe, iuris eminenter privati, dum sententia est res iuris publici quae absque dubio adscribi nequit inter negotia." — *Ibid.*, p. 44.* The writer disagrees with D'Angelo in his statement that *negotium* is the concern of canon 1680, for the authors quite generally understand judicial and extra-judicial acts as receiving mention in canon 1680. — Cf. Noval, *De Iudiciis*, n. 331; Vermeersch-Creusen, *Epitome*, III, n. 105; Feeney, *Restitutio in Integrum*, p. 121, note 41.

[50] Cf. D'Angelo, "De Restitutione in Integrum," *Periodica*, XVIII (1929), pp. 45*-48.* The writer agrees with Noone (*Nullity in Judicial Acts*, p. 111) when he states that too much stress should not be placed upon the footnotes of the Code; however, they at least give the interpretation placed on the canons by those responsible for drawing up these footnotes. Cf. also Seredi, "De valore iuridico fontium Codicis I.C.," *Jus Pontificium*, I (1921), 6366.

ed under canon 1892[51] contain references only to the judge, the parties involved in litigation, and their procurators. Moreover, the sources listed under canon 1894 are concerned only with the lack of the judicial summons.[52]

Other causes of nullity are not mentioned in these respective footnotes. On the other hand, the sources listed in the footnotes under canon 1905, §2, 4°, reflect various types of violations of the procedural law.[53] D'Angelo concluded from this consideration of canon 1905, §2, 4°, that the plea for a *restitutio in integrum* is to be employed for the purpose of attacking a sentence vitiated with other violations of procedural law. The plaint of nullity, however, was to be used against sentences vitiated with the defects mentioned in canon 1892 and 1894.[54]

Another argument which D'Angelo employed to include the violations of formal procedural law under the ruling of canon 1905,

[51] C. 41, C. II, q. 6; c. 22, X, *de officio et potestate iudicis delegati*, I, 29; c. 1, 3, 4, X, *de procuratoribus*, I, 38; c. 4, *de sententia et re iudicata*, II, 14, in VI°; Regulae servandae in iudiciis apud Suprem. Signaturae Ap. Tribunal, 6 mart. 1912, art. 4, c. — *AAS*, IV (1912), 189.

[52] C. 2, 4, 11, 12, C. III, q. 9; c. 10, X, *de sententia et re iudicata*, II, 27; c. 3, X, *ne sede vacante aliquid innovetur*, III, 9; S.C.C., *Lucana*, 2 et 16 dec. 1719 [*Fontes*, n. 3196]; *Albintimilien*, 18 iun. 1746 [*Fontes*, n. 3586]; *Tranen.*, 29 ian. 1859 [*Fontes*, n. 4172]; Lex propria S. R. Rotae et Signaturae Ap., 29 iun. 1908, can. 32, § 3 [*Fontes*, n. 6459]; Regulae servandae in iudiciis apud S. R. Rotae Tribunal, 4 aug. 1910, § 182 [*Fontes*, n. 6461]; Regulae servandae in iudiciis apud Suprem. Signaturae Ap. Tribunal, 6 mart. 1912, art. 4, a, art. 5 [*Fontes*, n. 6462].

[53] For example, c. 2, X, *ut lite non contestata non procedatur ad testium receptionem vel ad sententiam definitivam*, II, 6 [the issue was not joined]; C. 1, X, *de sententia et re iudicata*, II, 27 [the sentence was pronounced "*contra leges canonesque*"]; c. 15, X, *de purgatione canonica*, V, 34 [form of process was violated]; c. 5, X, *de feriis*, II, 9 [sentence was rendered on a forbidden day]; Benedictus XIV, const. *Ad militantis*, 30 mart. 1742, §43 [*Fontes*, n. 326—procedural forms when violated caused nullity of other acts]; S.C.C., *Premislien.*, 18 iun., 20 aug. 1887, ad 1 [*Fontes*, n. 427]; — nullity of sentence resulted from the use of unsworn witnesses and the exclusion of testimony]; Regulae servandae in iudiciis apud Suprem. Signaturae Ap. Tribunal. mart. 1912, art. 4, d, e. [*Fontes*, n. 6462 — neglect of law or an express violation of some law in force.]

[54] Cf. D'Angelo, "De Restitutione in Integrum," *Periodica*, XVIII (1929), p. 48*.

§2, 4°, is derived from the interpretation of canon 1905, §2, 4°, in the light of canon 18. In regard to the text and context of canon 1905, §2, 4°, the Code does not distinguish between law and law, but simply states "*legis praescriptum evidenter neglectum.*" If the Code does not distinguish, neither should we distinguish. Moreover, the plea for a *restitutio in integrum* was not granted as a remedy except in causes in which the ordinary remedies of appeal or the plaint of nullity could not be employed. D'Angelo seemed to imply that the plea for a *restitutio* could also be used in causes in which the plaint of nullity could have been employed.[55]

Considering the end or purpose of the law, D'Angelo stated that the plea for a *restitutio in integrum* serves as an extraordinary remedy against a sentence which cannot be attacked by means of an appeal or by way of the plaint of nullity. It seemed, therefore, that the Code should differentiate such causes clearly and expressly. Causes, then, in which the plea for a *restitutio in integrum* availed could not become clearly specified as long as authors continued to make fine distinctions and subdistinctions.[56]

D'Angelo argued from the *mens legislatoris* by stating that procedural laws are imposed by the legislator and must be followed, and that these various laws, if neglected, would have no remedy except the plea for a *restitutio in integrum*. After listing various canons to which canons 1892 and 1894 did not advert,[57] D'Angelo declared that it involves an injury to the law to maintain that the Code does not furnish any remedy against the neglect of these laws.

The proponents of the exclusive interpretation of canons 1892 and 1894 cite certain decisions of the Roman Tribunals as in agreement with their opinion. D'Angelo cited only two Rota decisions in support of his opinion.[58] In the decision of 1927, the Rota declared that the plea for a *restitutio in integrum* could be granted for violations of procedural law, and that the Code had reduced the causes of nullity to the ones specified in canons 1892

[55] Cf. D'Angelo, *ibid.*, p. 50.*

[56] Cf. D'Angelo, *ibid.*, p. 52.*

[57] Cf. canons 1585; 1587; 1595; 1596; 1731 etc. — *Periodica*, XVIII (1929), p. 54.*

and 1894.[59]

The writer agrees completely with this latter opinion as advanced by D'Angelo. The arguments given by the proponents of the exclusive interpretation of canons 1892 and 1894 seem sound and reasonable. The argument based on the *Schemata* of the Code is important. Although the violations of procedural law which resulted in an invalid process were listed in the various *Schemata,* the Code did not include these defects in canons 1892 and 1894.[60]

Another important argument for this opinion is found in the wording of the canons on the plaint of nullity against the sentence. Canon 1893, which grants the plaint of nullity against an irremediably invalid sentence, specifically refers to the causes of irremediable nullity as listed in canon 1892. This canon (1893) declares: "*nullitas de qua in can. 1892 proponi potest.*" The indication is that the plaint of nullity is to be employed against these irremediable nullities only. Furthermore, canon 1895 refers specifically to the cases of remediable nullity as expressed in canon 1894 — "*in casibus de quibus in can. 1894.*" The evident meaning, so it seems to the writer, is that the plaint of nullity can be used only against sentences vitiated with the defects specifically mentioned in canons 1892 and 1894.[62]

Moreover, Roberti states that the bishops expressed their desire to the preparatory commission of the Code that the number of nullities be curtailed.[63]

[58] S.R.R., *Restitutionis in integrum,* 8 apr. 1919 — *Decisiones,* XI (1919), 76-87; *S. Iacobi de Chile* (Restitutionis in Integrum et Compromissi), 5 iul. 1927, dec. XXXIV — *Decisiones,* XIX (1927), 276.

[59] Cf. S.R.R., *S. Iacobi de Chile,* 5 iul. 1927, coram R.P.D. Parrillo, dec. XXXIV — *Decisiones,* XIX (1927), 276-298. In this decision the Rota accepted D'Angelo's interpretation of the term *legis praescriptum.*

[60] Cf. *supra,* this Article, pp. 143-144.

[61] Cf. Feeney, *Restitutio in Integrum,* p. 121.

[62] Cf. Roberti, "Codicis iuris canonico Schemata de processibus," *Acta Congressus Iuridici Internationalis* 1934 (5 vols., Romae: Apud Custodiam Librarium Pont. Instituti Utriusque Iuris, 1935-1937), IV, 33.

[63] Cf. S.R.R., *Matriten,* (Nullitatis Actorum et Sententiae), 3 iul. 1933 coram R.P.D. Parrillo, dec. XLVIII, n. 2 — *Decisiones,* XXV (1933), 420-423; *Parisien,* (Nullitatis Matrimonii), 7 iun. 1934, coram R.P.D. Quattro-

Since the death of D'Angelo in 1930, the Sacred Rota has given a number of decisions, in addition to the two decisions already cited by D'Angelo, which espouse the opinion that canons 1892 and 1894 are all-inclusive in their listings of the nullifying defects in trials. That the jurisprudence of the Sacred Rota should support this opinion of D'Angelo is in accord with the present legislation. The history of the development of the plaint of nullity[64] clearly indicates the practice of the Holy See to curtail and limit the causes of nullities which affect the sentence. Moreover, the intent of the Code is to reduce invalid actions, invalid sentences, and all other forms of invalidity to the very minimum in matters pertaining to procedure.[65]

In concluding this discussion, the writer believes that the exclusive interpretation of canons 1892 and 1894 should be heartily welcomed. The sphere of the plaint of nullity is limited to the cases listed in canons 1892 and 1894, and the sphere of the plea for a *restitutio in integrum* serves simply to repair the injustice attaching to a *res iudicata* when such injustice has resulted from the neglect of any laws other than the provisions contained in canons 1892 and 1894.

calo, dec. XL, nn. 6, 7 — *Decisiones*, XXVI (1934), 349, 350; Querelae Nullitatis et Nullitatis Matrimonii, 8 febr. 1936, coram R.P.D. Jullien, dec. XII, n. 6 — *Decisiones*, XXVIII (1936), 119; *S. Iacobi de Chile* (Restitutionis in Integrum et Compromissi), 5 iul 1927, coram R.P.D. Parrillo, dec. XXXIV, n. 6 — *Decisiones*, XIX (1927), 280; *Tergestina* (Querelae Nullitatis et Nullitatis Matrimonii), 22 oct. 1936, coram R.P.D. Wynen, dec. LXV, n. 2 — *Decisiones*, XXVIII (1936), 621; *Rheginen.* (Nullitatis Matrimonii Incidentis), 16 iul. 1937, coram R.P.D. Teodori, dec. LI, n. 6 — *Decisiones*, XXIX (1937), 514; *Rheginen.* (Nullitatis Matrimonii Incidentis), 28 iul. 1938, coram R.P.D. Heard, dec. LI — *Decisiones*, XXX (1938), 472-477.

[64] Cf. *supra*, Chapters I and II. Especially Chapter II on the plaint of nullity from the sixteenth century.

[65] Cf. Doheny, *Canonical Procedure*, I, 124.

CONCLUSIONS

1. The plaint of nullity was first explicitly established by the Code of Canon Law as the proper remedy against a sentence vitiated with nullity. (Chapters I and II)

2. The absolute incompetence of the judge or the tribunal is determined by and limited to the enactments contained in canon 1556-1558. (pp. 48-50)

3. Religious, professed with solemn or simple vows, have no rightful standing in court, even as defendants, without the consent of their superiors; if they do otherwise, the sentence is vitiated with irremediable nullity. (pp. 71-72)

4. Unbaptized persons generally do not have any rightful standing in court in an ecclesiastical trial. The sentence concluding such a trial would be vitiated with irremediable nullity. (pp. 82-83.)

5. Baptized non-Catholics (apostates, heretics, and schismatics) are not directly denied a rightful standing in court. (pp. 84-86)

6. It is the omission of the initial summons of the defendant that renders a sentence invalid with a remediable nullity. (pp. 93-94)

7. The plaint of nullity as an exception amounts to a peremptory exception. It can be employed for the purpose of attacking irremediably as well as remediably invalid sentences. (pp. 111-114)

8. The judge delegated for a given trial (*ad causam*) has authority to receive the plaint of nullity against the sentence and to bring the process to a valid end. (pp. 126-128)

9. If the nullity of a sentence is sustained, the judge cannot independently of the will of the parties re-institute the process in causes that concern simply the private good. (p. 129)

10. In regard to remediably invalid sentences, the defender of the bond must combine the plaint of nullity as an accessory motive along with an appeal to attack a sentence which has sustained the plea of invalidity in any and all causes which demand the presence of this official. (pp. 132-133)

11. The listings in canons 1892 and 1894 are all-inclusive. The plaint of nullity against the sentence can look to only those defects which are therein delineated; it can not on its side invoke any other, even though similar, defects with any degree of judicial effectiveness. (pp. 143-148)

BIBLIOGRAPHY

Sources

Acta Apostolicae Sedis (*AAS*), Romae, 1909—

Acta Gregorii Papae, 4 vols., Romae, 1901-1904.

Bullarum Diplomatum et Privilegiorum Sanctorum Pontificum Taurinensis Editio, 24 vols. et Appendix, Augustae Taurinorum, Neapoli, 1857-1872.

Bullarii Romani Continuatio, 13 vols., Prati, 1845-1854.

Bullarii Romani Continuatio, 18 vols., Romae, 1835-1857.

Codex Iuris Canonici, Pii X Pontificis Maximi Iussu digestus Benedicti Papae XV auctoritate promulgatus, Romae, 1917.

Codicis Iuris Canonici Fontes, cura Emi Petri Card. Gasparri editi, 9 vols., Romae (postea Civitate Vaticana): Typis Polyglottis Vaticanis, 1923-1939 (Vols. VII-IX, ed. cura et studio Emi Iustiniani Card. Seredi).

Corpus Iuris Canonici, 2. ed. Lipsiensis, post Aemilii Ludovici Richteri curas instruxit Aemilius Friedberg, 2 vols., Lipsiae, 1879-1881.

Corpus Iuris Civilis, Vol. I, ed. stereotypa 15., *Institutiones* — recognovit P. Krueger; *Digesta* — recognovit Theodorus Mommsen, retractavit P. Krueger; Vol. II, ed. stereotypa 10., *Codex Iustinianus* — recognovit et retractavit P. Krueger; Vol. III, ed. stereotypa 5.. *Novellae Constitutiones* — R. Schoell; opus Schoelli morte interceptum absolvit G. Kroll, Berolini, 1928-1929.

Decretales D. Gregorii IX, una cum Glossis Restitutae, Romae, 1582.

Decretum Gratiani emendatum et notationibus illustratum, una cum glossis, Gregorii XIII Pont. Max. iussu editum, 2 vols., Romae, 1582.

Jaffe, P., *Regesta Pontificum Romanorum ab. condita Ecclesia ad annum post* Christum natum 1198, 2. ed. correctam et auctam auspiciis Gulielmi Wattenbach curaverunt F. Kaltenbrunner, P. Ewald, S. Loewenfeld, 2 vols., Lipsiae, 1885-1888.

Liber Sextus Decretalium D. Bonifacii Papae VIII suae integritati una cum Clementinis et extravagantibus earumque Glossis restitutus, Romae, 1582.

Monumenta Germaniae Historica, Gregorii I Papae, Registrum Epistularum, Tom. I et II, ediderunt P. Ewald et L. Hartmann, Berolini: Apud Weidmannos, 1891-1899.

Potthast, Augustus, *Regesta Pontificum Romanorum inde ab anno post Christum natum ad annum* 1304, 2 vols., Berolini, 1874-1875.

Sacrae Romanae Rotae Decisiones Recentiores, edd. Pr. Farinacius, Paulus Rubeus, Ioannes B. Compagnus, pro annis 1518-1684, 25 vols., Romae, 1618-1703; *Decisiones coram Pranetti*, Viterbii, 1839-1840; *Cursus Decisiones S.R.R.*, 5 vols. in 3, Romae, 1855.

Sacrae Romanae Rotae Decisiones seu Sententias ab anno 1909 — Romae: Typis Polyglottis Vaticanis, 1912—

REFERENCE WORKS

Altimarus, Blasius, *Tractatus de Nullitatibus in XIV Rubricas Divisus*, Neapoli, 1678.

Augustine, Charles, *A Commentary on the New Code of Canon Law*, 8 vols., Vol. VII, 3. ed., St. Louis, Mo.: B. Herder & Co., 1930.

Bartolus a Saxoferrato, *Commentarii*, Tomus VIII, *In Secudam atque Tertiam Codicis Partem*, Venetiis, 1590.

Beste, Udalricus, *Introduction in Codicem*, 3. ed., Collegeville, Minn.: St. John's Abbey Press, 1946.

Blat, Albertus, *Commentarium Textus Codicis Iuris Canonicim* Liber IV, *De Processibus*, Romae: Collegio Angelico, 1927.

Bouix, D., *Tractatus de Judiciis Ecclesiasticis*, 1. ed., 2 vols., Parisiis, 1855.

Bourque, John, *The Judicial Power of the Church*, The Catholic University of America Canon Law Studies, n. 337, Washington, D.C.: The Catholic University of America Press, 1953.

Bouvier, John, *Bouvier's Law Dictionary*, Baldwin's ed., Cleveland, Ohio: Banks- Baldwin Law Pub.: 1946.

Burke, Thomas J., *Competence in Ecclesiastical Tribunals*, The Catholic University of America Canon Law Studies, n. 14, Washington, D.C.: The Catholic University of America, 1922.

Cappello, Felix, *Summa Iuris Canonici*, Vol. III, editio altera. emendata et aucta, Romae: Apud Aedes Universitatis Gregorianae, 1940.

Connolly, Thomas, *Appeals*, The Catholic University of America Canon Law Studies, n. 79, Washington, D.C.: The Catholic University of America, 1932.

Coronata, Matthaeus Conte a, *Instituiones Iuris Canonici*, 5 vols., Vol. I-IV, 2. ed., 1939-1945; Vol. V, 1936, Romae, Marietti.

——, *Ius Publicum Ecclesiasticum*, 3. ed., Romae: Marietti, 1948.

——, *Compendium Iuris Canonici*, 2 vols., Taurini, 1938.

Coyle, Paul, *Judicial Exceptions*, The Catholic University of America Canon Law Studies, n. 193, Washington, D.C.: The Catholic University of America Pres, 1944.

De Luca, J. B., *Theatrum Veritatis et Iustitiae*, 16 vols. in 9, Coloniae Agrippinae, 1706.

Doheny, William J., *Canonical Procedure in Matrimonial Cases*, Vol. I, *Formal Judicial Procedure*, 2. ed., Milwaukee: The Bruce Publishing Co., 1948.

Dolan, John, *The Defensor Vinculi*, The Catholic University of America Canon Law Studies, n. 85, Washington, D.C.: The Catholic University of America, 1934.

Duerr, Charles J., *The Judicial Notary*, The Catholic University of America Canon Law Studies, n. 312, Washington, D.C.: The Catholic University of America Press, 1951.

Durandus, Gulielmus, *Speculum Iuris*, 3 vols., Venetiis, 1577.

Engel, L., *Collegium Universi Iuris Canonici*, 9. ed., Beneventi, 1760.

Feeney, Thomas, *Restitutio in Integrum*, The Catholic University of America Canon Law Studies, n. 129, Washington, D.C.: The Catholic University of America Press, 1941.

Gasparri, Petrus, Card., *Tractatus Canonicus de Matrimonio*, ed. nova ad mentem Codicis I.C., 2 vols., Typis, Polyglottis Vaticanis, 1932.

Glynn, Joseph, *The Promoter of Justice*, The Catholic University of America Canon Law Studies, n. 101, Washington, D.C.: The Catholic University of America, 1936.

Gonzalez-Tellez, Manuel, *Commentaria Perpetua in singulos textus quinque librorum Decretalium Gregorii IX*, 5 vols., Venetiis, 1756.

Goyeneche, *De Processibus*, Vol. I, Romae: Ad S. Ioannis Lat., pro manuscripto, 1950.

Hogan, James, *Judicial Advocates and Procurators*, The Catholic University of America Canon Law Studies, n. 133, Washington, D.C.: The Catholic University of America Press, 1941.

Hostiensis, Cardinalis (Henricus de Segusio), *Commentaria in Quinque Decretalium*, 5 vols., Venetiis, 1581.

——, *Summa Aurea*, Venetiis, 1570.

Kealy, John, *The Introductory Libellus in Church Court Procedure*, The Catholic University of America Canon Law Studies, n. 108, Washington, D.C.: The Catholic University of America, 1937.

Kilcullen, Thomas J., *The Collegiate Moral Person as Party Litigant*, The Catholic University of America Canon Law Studies, n. 251, Washington, D.C.: The Catholic University of America Press, 1947.

Krol, John J., *The Defendant in Contentious Trials*, The Catholic University of America Canon Law Studies, n. 146, Washington, D.C.: The Catholic University Press, 1942.

Lane, Loras, *Matrimonial Procedure in the Ordinary Courts of Second Instance*, The Catholic University of America Canon Law Studies, n. 253, Washington, D.C.: The Catholic University of America Press, 1947.

Lega, Michael, *Praelectiones De Iudiciis Ecclesiasticis*, 4 vols., Romae, 1896-1901; Vol. I, 2. ed., Romae, 1905.

——, *Commentarius in Iudicia Ecclesiastica iuxta Codicem Iuris Canonici*, 3 vols. and Appendix volume, ed. Bartoccetti, who also worte Appendix volume, Romae: Anonima Libreria Cattolica Italiana, 1950.

Lemieux, Delisle, *The Sentence in Ecclesiastical Procedure*, The Catholic University of America Canon Law Studies, n. 87, Washington, D.C.: The Catholic University of America, 1934.

Maranta, Robertus, *Speculum Aureum et Lumen Advocatorum*: *Praxis Civilis*, Venetiis, 1590.

Merkelbach, Benedictus, *Summa Theologicae Moralis*, 5. ed., 3 vols., Parisiis, 1947.

Metz, John, *The Recording Judge in the Ecclesiastical Collegiate Tribunal*, The Catholic University of America Canon Law Studies, n. 287, Washington, D.C.: The Catholic University of America Press, 1949.

McElroy, Francis J., *The Privileges of Bishops*, The Catholic University of America Canon Law Studies, n. 282, Washington, D.C.: The Catholic University of America Press, 1951.

Michiels, Gommarus, *Normae Generales Iuris Canonici*, 2 vols., Lublin, 1929.

Muniz, T., *Procedimientos Eclesiasticos*, 2. ed., 3 vols., Seville: Lib. de Sobrino de Izquierdo, 1926.

Noone, John J., *Nullity in Judicial Acts*, The Catholic University of America Canon Law Studies, n. 297, Washington, D.C.: The Catholic University of America Press, 1950.

Noval, J., *Commentarium Codicis Iuris Canonici*, Lib. IV, *De Processibus*, Pars I, *De Iudiciis*, Augustae Taurinorum: Marietti, 1920.

Ottaviani, Alaphridus, *Institutiones Iuris Publici Ecclesiastici*, Vol. I, *Ius Publicum Internum*, 3. ed., Romae: Typis Polyglottis Vaticanis, 1948.

Panormitanus (Nicholaus de Tudeschis), *Commentaria in Quinque Libros Decretalium*, 5 vols. in 7, Venetiis, 1588.

Pellegrini, Carolus, *Praxis Vicariorum et Omnium in Utroque Foro Iusdicentium*, Venetiis, 1706.

Pichler, Vitus, *Ius Canonicum secundum quinque Decretalium titulos Gregorii Papae IX practice explicatum*, 2 vols., Ravennae, 1741.

Pirhing, Ernricus, *Ius Canonicum in V Libros Decretalium*, ed. novissima, 4 vols., Dilingae, 1722.

Reiffenstuel, Anacletus, *Ius Canonicum Universum*, 5 vols. in 7, Parisiis, 1864-1870.

Roberti, Franciscus, *Codicis Iuris Canonici Schemata*, Lib. IV, *De Processibus*, Romae: Typis Polyglottis Vaticanis, 1940.

——, *De Processibus*, 2 vols., Romae: Apud Aedes Facultatis Iuridicae ad S. Apollinaris, 1926.

——, *De Processibus*, Vol. I, 2. ed., Romae: Apud Custodiam Librariam Pontificii Instituti Utriusque Iuris, 1941.

Rufinus, *Die Summa Decretorum des Magister Ruffnus*, ed. Henrich Singer, Paderborn, 1902.

Scaccia, Sigismundus, *Tractatus de Appellationibus*, 3. ed., Coloniae, 1717.

Schmalzgrueber, Franciscus, *Ius Ecclesiasticum Universum*, 5 vols., in 12, Romae, 1843-1845.

Schmier, Franciscus, *Ius Canonicum Universum*, Venetiis, 1754.

Stephanus Tornacensis, *Die Summa des Stephanus Tornacensis uber das Decretum Gratiani*, ed. J. F. Schulte, Giessen, 1891.

Vermeersch Arthurus–Creusen, Josephus, *Epitome Iuris Canonici*, 6. ed., 3 vols., Mechliniae-Romae: H. Dessain, 1937-1946.

Wenger, Leopold, *Institutes of the Roman Law of Civil Procedure*, revised ed. translated by Otis H. Fisk, New York: Veritas Press, 1940.

Wernz, Franciscus, *Ius Decretalium*, 6 vols. in 10, Romae et Prati, 1898-1914.

Wernz, F.-Vidal, P., *Ius Canonicum*, Vol. VI, *De Processibus*, 1927-1928; Vol. VII, *Ius Poenale*, 1937, Romae: Apud Aedes Universitatis Gregorianae.

——, *Internationalis*, 5 vols., Romae: Apud Custodiam Librariam Pont. Instituti Utriusque Iuris, 1935-1937, IV, 27-42.

Woywod, S., *A Practical Commentary on the Code of Canon Law*, revised and enlarged ed. by C. Smith, 2 vols., New York: Joseph F. Wagner, Inc., 1948.

ARTICLES

Cappello, Felix, "De acatholicorum incapacitate agendi in foro ecclesiastico," *Miscellanea Vermeersch*, 2 vols., Romae: Pontificiae Universita Gregoriana, 1935 — I, 393-402.

Crnica, A., "Defectus Codicis in designandis normis pro querela nullitatis," *Jus Pontificium*, XV (1935), 145-155.

D'Angelo, Sosio, "De restitutione in integrum iuxta canonem 1905, §2, 4°," *Periodica*, XVIII (1929), pp. 17*-62.*

Hanssen, Antonius, "De sanctione nullitatis in processu canonico," *Apollinaris*, XI (1923), 71-109; 215-263; XII (1939), 198-251.

Roberti, F., "Circa limites querele nullitatis et restitutionis in integrum," *Apollinaris*, I (1928), 476-483.

——, "Codicis Iuris Canonici schemata de processibus," *Acta Congressus Iuridici Internationalis*.

——, "De nullitate sententiae," *Apollinaris*, II (1929), 76-78.

Serédi, "De valore iuridico fontium Codicis I.C.," *Jus Pontificium*, I (1921), 63-66.

Woywod, S., "Procedural Law of the Church," *The Homiletic and Pastoral Review*, XXX (1930), pp. 725-732.

PERIODICALS

Analecta Iuris Pontificii, Romae, 1855-1869; Parisiis, 1872-1891.

Apollinaris, Romae, 1928—

Archiv für katholisches Kirchenrecht (*AKKR*), Innsbruck, 1857-1861; Mainz, 1862—

Jus Pontificium, Romae, 1921-1940.

The Homiletic and Pastoral Review, New York, 1900—

Periodica de Religiosis et Missionariis, Brugis, 1905-1919; ab anno 1920: *Periodica de Re Canonica et Morali utilia praesertim Religiosis et Missionariis*, Brugis, 1920-1927; *Periodica de Re Morali, Canonica, Liturgica*, Brugis, 1927-1936, et Romae, 1937—

ABBREVIATIONS

AAS — *Acta Apostolicae Sedis*
ASS — *Acta Sanctae Sedis*
Bull. Rom. — *Bullarium Romanum*
Bull. Rom. Cont. — *Bullarii Romani Continuatio*
C — *Codex*
D — *Digestum*
Decisiones — *S. Romanae Rotae Decisiones seu Sententiae*
Fontes — *Codicis Iuris Canonici Fontes*
Jaffe — *Regesta Pontificium Romanorum* (edited by Ewald, Kaltenbrunner, Loewenfeld)
MGH — *Monumenta Germaniae Historica*
N — *Novellae*
Periodica — *Periodica de Religiosis et Missionariis etc.*
Pont. Comm. Interp. — *Pontificia Commissio ad Codicis Canones authentice interpretandos*
Potthast — *Regesta Pontificium Romanorum*
S.C.C. — Sacra Congregatio Concilii
S.C.S.Off. — Sacra Congregatio Sancti Officii
S.R.R. — Sacra Romana Rota

ALPHABETICAL INDEX

BIOGRAPHICAL NOTE

William Thomas Curtin was born November 21, 1921, in Leavenworth, Kansas. He received his elementary and secondary education in the Cathedral Grade School and Immaculata High School in that city. After graduating from high school, he attended St. Benedict's College in Atchison, Kansas, graduating from that institution in April, 1943, with a degree of Bachelor of Arts. In September of 1943 he entered Kenrick Seminary in St. Louis, Missouri. He was ordained to the priesthood on January 19, 1947. He was assigned to St. Peter's Church in Kansas City, Kansas, which in 1947 became the Cathedral of the diocese. In 1952 this diocese was elevated to the status of an archdiocese. He served as a member of the Cathedral staff, in Kansas City, Kansas, until he commenced the study of Canon Law in October, 1952, at the Catholic University of America, where he received the degree of Baccalaureate in Canon Law in June, 1953, and the degree of Licentiate in Canon Law in June, 1954.

CANON LAW STUDIES*

358. Sesto, Rev. Gennaro J., S.D.B., A.B., S.T.L., J.C.L., Guardians of the mentally ill in ecclesiastical trials.
359. Carroll, Rev. James J., A.B., J.C.L., The bishop's quinquennial report.
360. Curtin, Rev. William Thomas, A.B., J.C.L., The plaint of nullity against the sentence.
361. Ganter, Rev. Bernard J., J.C.L., Clerical attire.
362. Goertz, Rev. Victor M., J.C.L., the judicial summons.
363. Heintschel, Rev. Donald E., A.B., J.C.L., The mediaeval concept of an ecclesiastical office.
364. Kelliher, Rev. Jeremiah Francis, S.A., A.B., S.T.L., J.C.L., Loss of privileges.
365. Mock, Rev. Timothy, C.M.M., J.C.L., Disqualification of electors in ecclesiastical elections.
366. Smyer, Rev. Francis Anthony, A.B., J.C.L., Canonical regulations regarding exposition of the Blessed Sacrament according to canons 1274 and 1275.
367. Wiggins, Rev. Urban C., A.B., J.C.L., Property laws of the State of Ohio affecting the Church.

* For a complete list of the available numbers of this series apply to the Catholic University of America Press, 620 Michigan Ave., N.E., Washington 17, D.C., for a general catalogue.

www.ingramcontent.com/pod-product-compliance
Lightning Source LLC
LaVergne TN
LVHW041115090826
844660LV00060B/486
9780813225272